Little Stories of Your Life

TO RUTH, WHOSE STORY ENDED FAR
TOO SOON. I WILL ALWAYS MISS YOU.

TO D, S, R & E. I LOVE YOU
BEST IN ALL THE WORLD.

Publishing Director Sarah Lavelle
Senior Commissioning Editor Harriet Butt
Commissioning Editor Sarah Thickett
Copy Editor Sarah Mitchell
Proofreader Catherine Jackson
Senior Designer Gemma Hayden
Photographer Laura Pashby
Head of Production Stephen Lang
Production Controller Sabeena Atchia

English Language edition published in 2021 by Quadrille,
an imprint of Hardie Grant Publishing
Quadrille
52–54 Southwark Street
London SE1 1UN
quadrille.com

Cataloguing in Publication Data: a catalogue record for this book
is available from the British Library.

ISBN 978 1 78713 711 0
Printed in China

Little Stories of Your Life

Find your voice, share your world and tell your story

Words and photos by

LAURA PASHBY

QUADRILLE

'ALWAYS BE ON THE LOOKOUT
FOR THE PRESENCE
OF WONDER.'

E.B. WHITE

Contents

Introduction

The little stories of our lives tell of simple moments when the everyday is transformed into something remarkable. The magic of sunlight dancing across a bedroom wall after days of relentless grey; swirling frost patterns etched onto a kitchen window on a cold morning; or an envelope dropping unexpectedly onto the doormat, the address written in a familiar, beloved hand. Little stories are small, but they shine bright: like fireflies, or sparkling water droplets on a winter branch. They concern the people that we love, the details that we observe, the small secrets that we keep and the memories that make us glow inwardly. Little stories encapsulate the reasons we get out of bed in the morning: they describe the tiny pleasures and commonplace rituals that see us through every day. These are stories of moments that we share, moments that we quietly treasure and that somehow make us who we are.

If we don't see the value of tiny moments, we will miss the little stories. If we fail to notice them, they will fly, unobserved, into the ether, but if we learn to pay attention, we can gather them up and keep them close. We can catch them as they drift by in the sleepy afternoon air. We can sense them (like voices echoing quietly just beyond the path) and we can follow their whisper. There is always a little story around the corner of the day. We meet them on the back seat of the bus, we come across them as we fold ourselves into a favourite chair in a quiet café corner, or we find them tucked gently into the pages of a well-loved book. Little stories surprise us, on snowy mornings or rainy afternoons. We discover them when we find something forgotten in a pocket, they flutter out as we draw open the curtains on a sunny morning, or we unearth them hidden at the back of a drawer. Capturing and recording the little stories of our lives involves consciously slowing down. It means stopping to notice ordinary moments and familiar details. Telling the little stories of our lives is about cherishing what truly matters to us, making memories; capturing life creatively, and finding out what makes us who we are.

I've spent the past decade using words and photographs to tell the little stories of my own life, during which time I've developed my creativity and built a new career. I've changed the way I see the world and the way I see myself. This storytelling journey of mine began on the day that, as a new mother (tired, a little bored and lacking in confidence), I started a blog. When I made the decision to begin to tell the little stories of my life, I began to see my everyday with fresh eyes and stopped feeling that I had nothing interesting to say. I learned to look for moments of beauty or poignancy, to seek out small stories and to celebrate the charms of the apparently mundane. I took the opportunity to explore my creativity on my own terms and, in the process, I shared the story of my life – the changing vignettes of my kitchen table, my love of craft and books, and the details of the world I saw around me. I made connections and built friendships with other storytellers. My blog led me to

Instagram and, in time, to opportunities: to write for magazines and websites, to collaborate with brands and to sell my photographs, allowing me to build myself a freelance career with storytelling at its heart. I truly believe that everything that followed came from finding the confidence to believe that my stories were worth sharing and my quiet voice was relevant. I do what I love, I've found who I am, and it all began with little stories.

You may feel, as I did, that making your voice heard in a loud world is challenging and that telling your own story feels intimidating. In this book, I will show that you too can access the innate strength of your little stories through creative, mindful and thoughtful storytelling methods. You can find time to preserve the moments that matter in your life and you can use your stories to connect with other people. To begin a storytelling practice you need nothing more than a camera, paper and a writing implement so, as you turn the pages of this book, consider having to hand a camera of some sort (your phone camera would be perfect), as well as a pencil and a notebook. Notebook, journal, diary and scrapbook are different words for what is essentially the same thing: a place to write down our little stories. Whether you write on paper or in a document saved to a laptop or phone, whether you jot down snippets of ideas and half-formed sentences or transcribe a full daily account, it all comes from the same impulse – to remember and to record. In this book I will use the words 'journal' and 'notebook' interchangeably. Journalling can sound like an intimidatingly soul-searching practice, but in essence it is simply writing in a notebook. Like many things it is most effective when it becomes a regular habit – I would suggest aiming to jot down a little story in your journal each day – but don't be disheartened if you skip a day, or days. Together, your little stories will nevertheless add up to a much bigger picture.

Little stories can seem like nothing, but they mean everything. They surprise us, they delight us, they even sometimes break our hearts. I believe that by using words and photographs to record the little stories of our lives, we can each create a patchwork of tiny tales and begin to build a sense of our overarching life story, which reveals something of who we really are. If you gather together the precious fragments that make up *your* life and hold those fragments to the light, looking for the little stories within, what will you see?

I want to encourage you to think not just about *how* you can tell your little stories, but also to reflect on *why* you might choose to do so.

I hope that this book will encourage you to view your world a little differently, helping you to find your unique creative voice and to develop the habit of capturing precious moments of your everyday. Your stories are waiting to be told and the details of your life matter. Telling the little stories of your life can open your world to new connections, to beauty and to opportunity – this book will show you how.

The Magic of
the Everyday

You have stories to tell.

You have stories to tell, and you're ready to tell them. I know that you have stories to tell because we all do, every one of us – it's the truth of being human. I know that you're ready to tell them because you've picked up this book. I'd like to guide you on a gentle storytelling journey. Will you walk with me? Storytelling begins with paying attention. When my middle son was a baby, I came across a poem by Mary Oliver called *Sometimes*, in which she prescribes three instructions for living: 'Pay attention. / Be astonished. / Tell about it.'[1] I read the poem again and again. I could feel my heart beating. Those simple phrases felt like everything to me: a distillation, a revelation, an invitation, a challenge, a mantra that I have carried with me ever since. Every word that I write, every picture that I take, every story that I tell comes from the act of paying attention. When something fascinates (or astonishes) me, I have the urge to record and sometimes to share – to tell about it. Attention is where storytelling begins, and paying attention is about finding focus. The world is full of noise, both literal and digital, and it can seem as if everything and everyone are competing to be heard. Your attention is like a blessing that reveals and transforms anything it touches. What it alights on is up to you. The closer you look at the world around you and the more deeply you perceive the details of your life, the more that you will find to wonder at.

In our kitchen, we have an oval Victorian drop-leaf table. It has been in the family since my father-in-law was a child, if not before, and it has seen a good deal of living and a number of homes over the years. The table is definitely past its best, marked by mug stains, pen lines, fading and scuffs. Each scar on its surface has a story to tell: the burn from a hot enamel casserole dish filled with soup for a Saturday lunch; the felt tip pen that spilled over the edges of a child's drawing; the dings and dents of cutlery carelessly thrown down; the varnish worn away by the wiping of a hundred cloths. Old, but not an antique, distressed (but not artfully), seen but not noticed, this tired old table is very much at the heart of our home. During its decades standing solidly at the family's core, the table has borne witness to whole lifetimes. Its truth, were it able to speak, would be the daily life of many branches of our family – the secrets of the home – stories that are simple and domestic, but timeless too.

One day in the autumn, a decade ago, I was sitting at this kitchen table nursing a cup of tea, my laptop open on the table nestled amongst stray toys, the debris of breakfast, a basket of apples and a pile of unopened letters. Looking after my young children was wonderful but I found it relentlessly exhausting; there barely seemed to be time for me to take a breath of my own, let alone have a thought. Some days felt like an endless treadmill of feeding, changing, soothing and tidying, all whilst diplomatically negotiating a path through the tantrums and strange logic of toddlerhood. I loved my life, but I was feeling overwhelmed by it, as if I had become submerged by the tide of motherhood. On that day, the internet offered me a lifeline. I realized that in order to rediscover my sense of self, I wanted to find a way to tell the stories of my life, however mundane they might seem: I decided to start an online journal – a blog. My first post began with what I saw right there on the table in front of me – a basket of apples from my neighbour's tree. An unexpected gift, a tiny kindness, a little story waiting to be told.

Storytelling requires only a few simple tools. As you read this book, you will find it helpful to keep a notebook and a pen nearby (or, if you prefer the digital route, a note-taking app on your phone). If a beautiful, pristine notebook feels intimidating to you, chose a cheap flimsy exercise book so that you will feel less pressure to fill its pages with wisdom or beauty. Do you still feel intimidated? Skip past the first page and begin writing on the second or third page. This journal is yours. Take back your writing from school, university or work, whenever you last had your efforts marked and maybe found wanting. Words are yours to use as you choose – in sentences or not, neatly or otherwise. Don't think about writing as something you are or are not 'good' at, but as something that belongs to you: a path from your heart to the page.

In order to tell our little stories, we will be using a combination of words and photographs. Photography is not just an incredibly powerful storytelling medium, it's also an increasingly accessible one. My own first real experience of photography was on my fifteenth birthday when my Dad gave me an Olympus Trip 35mm film camera and set up a darkroom in our tiny downstairs cloakroom. I found myself entranced by the alchemy of film photography. Each image that I composed through the viewfinder of the camera was a carefully considered leap in the dark, a picture that wouldn't be seen until I lifted the negatives from the tray and saw the inverse images swim into focus. I will always love the unique tones and emotional resonance of shooting on film and the process of developing the images, but nowadays almost all of my images are digital and many of them are shot using the camera on my phone. Phone cameras are the perfect tool for telling little stories because we carry them everywhere, there's no limit to the number of images that we take and we can see as we shoot what an image looks like, allowing us to make adjustments as we go. Throughout this book, I will be guiding you to use your phone camera (or another camera, if you prefer) and your journal to record little stories of everyday moments.

It's no secret that the most challenging part of storytelling is often knowing where to begin. I'd like to suggest that we start small, as small as possible, taking inspiration from what may well be beside you right at this very moment. Let's begin with a cup of tea. A cup of tea (or whatever hot drink you prefer – it's your choice) is such a simple everyday item. If you're like me, you drink several of them each day, whether sipped scalding hot, or made, forgotten, rediscovered and gulped down – lukewarm but still welcome. Any cup of tea can contain a multitude of stories.

Firstly, there's the cup. Perhaps it's your favourite cup. It might be chipped from daily use, or new and immaculate. Your cup may have been a souvenir from a trip or a holiday, a gift, or a treasured purchase from an artisan potter. What's in your cup, I wonder? Tea, coffee, herbal tea? Are you cutting down on dairy and substituting oat milk? Did you add sugar for an energy boost? Do you like your hot drinks weak or strong? Your cup of tea is the story of a moment – *this* moment – when you picked it up to drink. Where are you drinking: home, at your own kitchen table, or are you in a café, perched on a park bench, in an office, or a waiting room? How do you feel as you sip your drink: are you revived, hydrated, comforted or encouraged? Do you have your drink at a certain time of day? (My Yorkshire granny had a cup of coffee at precisely ten in the morning, every day for most of her nine decades.) Is anyone sharing this cuppa with you, or is it a moment of solitude? The details that make your cup of tea and your moment unique are the tiny building blocks of this particular little story.

My cup of tea is strong but milky; it sits on top of a pile of books on the desk in my tiny attic office. I have woken up early to write whilst the rest of the household is still sleeping. The only sounds I can hear are birdsong and the crisp rustling of the huge beech tree in the garden opposite; its leaves sound like the whisper of ocean waves, just out of sight. I'm drinking hot Yorkshire tea from a small, blue-and-white-striped mug that I bought several years ago on a trip

ANY CUP OF TEA CAN CONTAIN
A MULTITUDE OF STORIES.

to Laugharne (a misty, mystical town, once home to the poet Dylan Thomas). This mug is a replica of the one that Dylan Thomas kept on the desk in his writing shed: a wooden room dappled by pools of light, with views of the estuary, fading photographs pinned to the walls and crumpled paper scattered on the floor. My own mug is chipped now, its glaze cracked and faded, but I love it because it reminds me of Dylan Thomas's poetry – the way in which he tumbled words together to conjure images and meanings that are startling and beautiful. I don't truly believe that any of the magic of his writing will transfer via our matching mugs from his desk to mine, but as I sit down at my laptop for another day's work, I take pleasure in sipping my tea from a poet's mug.

A cup of tea is a popular visual motif. It has aesthetic appeal – the familiar, curved shape of the mug, the rising steam – but more importantly, a cup of tea has universality: it's visual shorthand for a moment of peace and comfort. This simple ritual can be represented with endless variation, but we all understand its essence. There may be hands cradling the mug, a posy of flowers on the table, a book, discarded breakfast bowls, a newspaper or a slice of cake. The same everyday little story is told in a thousand different ways, one of which is yours. I'd like to invite you to record your cup of tea, by snapping a picture on your phone, writing a descriptive paragraph in your journal, or ideally both. Remember to start by paying close attention: record the fleeting moment and tell the particular story of this cup of yours.

Something I have learned from my decade of storytelling is that there's *magic* in the everyday. A quiet glimmer that's always there, although we often neglect to notice it, caught up as we are in the busy business of living – shopping lists and to do lists, the places we go, the people we see. Our daily lives are filled with what Joan Didion called 'ordinary blessings', blessings which we tend to take for granted, not realizing until we risk losing them that they are the most precious bounty we possess. There is a tension between the ordinary, which we overlook, and the extraordinary, which we are endlessly seeking. As writer Dani Shapiro puts it: 'If I dismiss the ordinary – waiting for the special, the extreme, the extraordinary to happen – I may just miss my life.'[2] Sometimes we just need to look more closely to realize that, amongst life's minutiae, magic hides.

I find magic in the gossamer touch of sunlight on my morning pillow, in the sound of milk bottles clinking in the dawn. I see it in the opening of a window, as I breathe for the first time that year the earthy scent of approaching spring, or in the glimpse of a cloud-scattered sky reflected in the surface of a puddle. Everyday magic will mean something different to each of us, but it's there in the moments that are nothing and everything, all at once. It's a sparkling thread woven through the days of our lives.

The daily choices we make – our tasks, routines and necessary interactions – show what matters to us and indirectly reveal something of ourselves. The author Annie Dillard wrote that 'How we spend our days is, of course, how we spend our lives'.[3] A life is made up of many, many days, all stitched together. The ordinary is not something to be dismissed or ignored: the everyday is everything. Small moments accumulate, bound together like patchwork into a pattern that is unique for each of us, making us who we are. Can you slow down, just a little and open your eyes to the possibility of everyday magic? Pay close attention and you may catch an unexpected glimpse of something extraordinary hidden within the ordinary – like a luminescent pearl nestled inside an unremarkable oyster shell.

Begin with a List

In order to fully experience the little moments of our lives – and the everyday magic of the world around us – we begin by noticing and then recording. A list is the simplest place to start. Lists are a condensed form of storytelling that help us to focus thoughts and attention. They are a quick way in which to record feelings, sense impressions, observations or thoughts.

To begin with, just aim to list five things you've noticed, but of course you can add more if you want to. When compiling ideas for lists, it's helpful to tune in to your senses. Some possible lists could be:

- Sounds I can hear
- *Blue* things I noticed today (or use any colour as appropriate)
- What I have tasted today
- Scents that remind me of home
- Moments when I felt happy today
- Textures that I saw as I walked
- Spots where the sunlight touches the walls in my home
- My current favourite words
- Signs of the season (e.g. summer) that I noticed today

A list is a good starting point for writing because it is easy, fast and non-threatening. If you feel overwhelmed by an experience that you are looking to describe, or a story that you are wishing to tell, begin with a quick list of words that describe it or that you associate with it. Writing lists is an excellent way to gather topics and ideas for longer pieces of journal writing or storytelling. You can write many short lists, or you could dedicate a page in your journal (or a notes file on your phone) to a particular list – e.g. 'moments of everyday magic' – of things that you observe and add to over time.

EVERYDAY MAGIC WILL MEAN
SOMETHING DIFFERENT TO EACH
OF US, BUT IT'S THERE IN THE
MOMENTS THAT ARE NOTHING AND
EVERYTHING, ALL AT ONCE.

In this busy, connected world, the perils of comparison are ever present, particularly if we spend our time lost on social media. Other people's lives can appear to be perfect and filled with successes: it's easy to feel that our own lives are not enough, that we have nothing to offer, no story worth sharing. I know from experience, however, that behind the glossy facade of every aspirational Instagram image is hidden the messy imperfection of real life. A single picture only ever tells one part of someone's story and it's natural to want to showcase the best of ourselves. Rather than getting drawn in to the stories of others and feeling yourself lacking, I want to help you to look for ways in which to tell the stories that *you* will want to remember, stories that belong to you and to you alone – your *own* little stories.

You have stories to tell.

Imagine that you're viewing yourself through a movie camera. The camera starts with a wide shot that shows everything that's going on in your village, town or city. Zoom in to focus on where you are now – your house, or the café or the park bench where you currently sit. Zoom in closer, so that we're focused just on you, reading this book. Zoom even further and find a detail that draws your eye or tugs on your heart. It might be something that's part of the room or space in which you sit. Perhaps it's a sweet inscription on the park bench or the familiar cracks in the arm of a leather armchair? It might be a hole in the sleeve of your favourite jumper, your hair tucked behind your ear, or the scuffed shoes that you kicked off before you curled up your legs and folded your feet under you. Perhaps it's an old train ticket that you're using as a bookmark. There is something specific about where you are right now that tells of who you are in this moment. Focus on what it is and why it speaks to you. What does this detail have to say to you? How does it make you feel? This is a little story just waiting to be told.

The joy of these stories is that they are *little*. You don't have to tell the story of your whole year, week or even day – you can choose to tell the stories of the moments you want to remember, the instants that mean something to you. From the humdrum to the revelatory, little stories concern the things that bring us a flash of happiness, that speak to us or give us pause. They are about creating a record of our days: our homes and routines, the way we move through the world, the things that call to us, the people that we love and the way in which only we see them. Little stories are about finding magic in the mundane – things that make our hearts sing, details that are usually overlooked. Small doesn't equate to insignificant: all these little stories add up to the narrative tide that carries us all.

Collecting together just one moment from each day adds up over the course of weeks and months to a portrait of a life, one that encapsulates the changing seasons and the passage of time, a personal record and an accumulation of memories that is utterly unique. Taking just one photograph a day creates a collection of images that tells the stories of a life. Daily photography is also the best way to train your photographic eye and to teach yourself to see your world through the prism of creative composition. It has even been scientifically proven to improve wellbeing through (among other benefits) self-care and the potential for reminiscence.[4]

My own visual storytelling journey began when I set myself what was called a '365 challenge': I decided to take one photograph every day. I didn't share the images, I compiled them together on my phone. It was the process, not the end product, that mattered to me at that time. I was learning to pay attention, training my eye to look for little stories as I moved through each day. I found that, as time went by, it became much easier to see one or more interesting little stories in even what felt like the dullest of days. I was digging for everyday magic and I began to find it. In the process, my creative eye and photography skills improved exponentially and I felt happier too.

Set Yourself an Everyday Photography Challenge

As you turn the pages of this book, set yourself your own everyday photography challenge. You could take a photograph every day for a year or, if that feels too much, you could do it for a month, or just a week. You might combine this with daily journalling; if you print out your photographs, or shoot with an instant camera, you could stick your photographs into your journal. You may wish to give your photography challenge a theme, for example: food; finding something colourful; mornings; capturing the weather. Choose the timescale and the theme that work for you. By opening your eyes to little stories as you move through your days, you will begin to notice moments of everyday magic and think about how you can capture them.

When you have completed your challenge – at the end of the week, month or year – take a little time to reflect on any patterns that you might notice in what you have chosen to photograph. Do you observe any changes to how you feel or the way that you see after trying this exercise?

Magic is found in the overlooked details that we take for granted, and we can teach ourselves to see beyond the surface and find meaning, truth or wonder in quotidian events. If we look more closely at the everyday we may see glimpses of the eternal.

A simple moment – seeing someone you love off in the morning with a kiss, walking down the street in the sunshine or hanging up your coat as you return home after a long day – contains echoes of that moment at other points in your life and in lives that have gone before. We are all part of an endlessly intricate spiderweb of stories woven together with interconnecting threads. When we read or watch the stories of others, our sense of recognition is sparked not by wild adventures, but by simple moments. The unremarkable ways in which others people's lives mirror our own can allow us to feel closer to them, engendering a tug of recognition and of sympathy. Our little stories are unique, but they are also universal.

Everyday magic will mean something different for each of us, but if we choose to look for it, there are common moments in which it can often be found.

QUIET MOMENTS
There is magic in quiet moments because we allow ourselves time just to be. A quiet moment could be a bowl of porridge eaten in a dawn kitchen; an empty seat on the morning commute; a few minutes reading a book at a bus stop; a lunchtime walk through the park and a sandwich on a bench; a hot bath at the end of a long day. Quiet moments allow us to be alone with our thoughts. They are often rare, which makes them all the more precious. The story of a quiet moment draws us in because for many of us, momentary peace is a precious commodity.

MOMENTS OF DOMESTICITY
Easily overlooked, often begrudged – moments of domesticity can reveal fleeting glimpses of everyday magic. The foamy dance

of soap suds in the washing up bowl; crisp laundry blowing in the breeze against a blue sky; small muddy boots lined up outside the door; the flour dust that litters the table as biscuits are being baked. Finding the magic in recurring domestic chores and routines can change the way that we think about them for the better.

MOMENTS OF CONNECTION

There are moments in our days when we feel connection to another person, whether absent or present. Holding a small child's hand on the way to school; reading an email from a friend who lives far away; picking up a brooch that once belonged to a grandmother; sharing an evening meal with a partner. These are moments we will want to remember, where our little stories cross over with the stories of those we love.

MOMENTS OF ESCAPE

Sometimes, a moment in the day transports us from the here and now to a place of memory, imagination or dream. It might be an object or photograph that reminds us of someone or somewhere that we love. It could be a novel, a podcast or a film. Perhaps an advert on the side of a bus sets us dreaming of faraway shores. The magic of these moments is that they provide escape and respite, even if it's just in the imagination.

TIMELESS MOMENTS

Timeless moments are ones that reflect back to us past stories, connecting us to days and lives that have gone before. Moments of quiet significance or family ritual, such as the baking of a birthday cake, a table set for tea on a grandmother's cloth, a favourite weekend breakfast or a walk in a special place. They can be traditions or everyday things that are part of a thread of history. These moments contain magic because they are stories that continue to be lived and told over and over again.

MOMENTS OF DOMESTICITY CAN
REVEAL FLEETING GLIMPSES
OF EVERYDAY MAGIC.

Capturing Breakfast

I'd like to begin this exercise in the way that you begin your day: with breakfast. For this task you will take one to three images of your breakfast.

- Light is the photographer's most important tool and one golden rule of photography is to try and take your images in natural daylight rather than artificial light, if you can. If it's possible, turn off the overhead light, or if you are in a café, choose a table by a window. Take note of where the daylight is coming from and observe how it touches your breakfast scene. What does it highlight? Can you position yourself so that you avoid harsh shadows in your image?

- Make a conscious choice about the angle at which you will be holding your camera to take your image. You could hold it flat above the breakfast scene for an overhead shot, flat and straight in front of the scene, or at a three-quarter angle, mirroring your perspective as you sit to eat. Experiment with angles until you find the one that best captures this little story.

- There is a simple rule of photography called the 'rule of odds'. This means that when you create an image you should consider including an odd-numbered group of key items, for instance a cup, a bowl, a spoon. Groups of three, or other odd numbers, are naturally pleasing to the eye.

- Take something out: images often tell a story best when they are uncluttered. See how the image changes if you move one or two items out of shot.

- It's okay to be messy. You're telling the story of this moment, of your breakfast. The crumbs on the table, the porridge on the spoon, the spilt sugar… these all tell something of the moment and draw the viewer in. Look for signs of life and make them part of your image.

- Remember to focus the camera on what you see as the most important part of your image. With most phone cameras you tap on the screen to focus.

- Shoot with your heart. Notice your feelings as you tell the story of this breakfast scene.

Why not capture your breakfast every day for a week and notice what changes and what remains the same from day to day?

There's a secret to composing a little story that is full of meaning and resonates with the reader. The secret? Telling something true. Telling something true can feel intimidating – as if you will be laying yourself bare – but there's a difference between a truth and a secret. Little stories don't call for earth-shattering revelations, they just need a kernel within them that has meaning to you. A story doesn't have to be about what you can see; a story can be about how you feel. The moments when an emotion or idea clarifies in your head, when you observe a sense of connection to a place or a person, when you recognize the significance or beauty of a particular object – when you think *yes, this is how it feels to be me, right here and right now*. Those are moments when you have a little story to tell.

The stories of *your* life will encompass an element of your uniqueness – a glimpse of who it is that you are – and this makes each little story more potent. Telling something true is a subtle art – you can do so by showing, rather than overtly telling. A little story can obliquely reveal a truth: the things that are meaningful and important in your life are communicated by what you choose to share. For example, I compose and share images of myself in the woods, particularly in the mist. On the surface, these images are about my enjoyment of walking, particularly on a foggy morning, but they also show my love of solitude (I'm an introvert and having regular time alone allows me to thrive). Being outside in nature, particularly in the woods, is an escape, one that is crucial to my emotional wellbeing – something which I've understood in greater depth since I began to explore and capture my experiences among the trees with my camera and with my words. Amongst the trees, I am most truly myself.

As human beings, our lives can be seen as an ongoing search for meaning and our little stories are a good place to start. Sometimes the bigger picture – or the wider truth – starts to become apparent when we look more closely. Unexpected connections and underlying meaning can be found through the process of gathering together elements of life that we find notable, or that connect us in some way to a deeper sense of feeling. It may be that in telling your little stories you will discover a wider unknown; but that revelation begins with one little story – it begins by telling something true.

It's truth, I have learned, that draws people into a story. A tale can be incredibly powerful when it's shared with honesty, but truth can also make us feel vulnerable. Starting small helps: we're not telling our whole life stories, we're telling *little* stories of our lives. Sharing the truth about one tiny moment feels much less intimidating than relating significant events, and yet even a tiny truth will create a connection between the storyteller and the viewer or reader. A small story told truly will always have more power than a grandiose narrative told without heart.

The story that I told that first day on my blog was the little story of a basket of apples. In those days, I lived in a Victorian terraced house in Bristol. My favourite room in the house was the attic, from which I had a view across the city's rooftops and the row of gardens below. From my attic window I watched the clouds pass by, but I also gazed at the gnarled old apple tree in the garden next door. In the springtime, it produced a cloud of delicate white blossom which would drift down like confetti into the garden below. In the autumn, it was laden with glossy red fruit which I could see but not touch. Those beautiful, unattainable apples reminded me of a once-beloved picture book: the fairy tale in which Rapunzel's mother gazes at the forbidden fruits of the garden next door, pining for them but unable to pick them. One day, unexpectedly, the neighbours to whom the tree belonged left on my doorstep a basket of those very same apples. Delighted, I baked a cake with the longed-for fruit (which was every bit as delicious as I had dreamed it would be) cutting slices for my small sons and handing slices over the fence to the kind couple next door.

This was the little story of the basket of apples. It was the smallest, simplest story, but it was mine, and it was true.

Telling little stories is not necessarily about commemorating notable events such as trips, celebrations or parties. It's finding a story to tell, however small, on a normal day. Sometimes this can be a real struggle on a rainy Wednesday in winter, when you feel that there's nothing interesting taking place in your life, but the days that seem the least noteworthy still have tiny tales waiting to be told and the rewards are greatest when you find some hidden magic. In any life there will be joy and sorrow, celebration and heartbreak, but it's the stretches of time in between that matter: the beautiful, ordinary days. When we tell the stories of our lives, we don't need a grand narrative arc. I'm not suggesting that you pen an epic novel, and your stories do not have to be confined to bright, exciting events. I want to encourage you to tell your own story by starting small and telling the *little stories of your life*.

It's time to begin paying attention.

A SMALL STORY TOLD TRULY WILL
ALWAYS HAVE MORE POWER THAN
A GRANDIOSE NARRATIVE TOLD
WITHOUT HEART.

Being in the Moment

Attention is a scarce commodity.

We don't give it, we pay it, as if it were a form of currency. In the eyes of marketers and brands, attention translates to money. Their aim is to capture or to grab it, hence the endless bombardment of advertising that we see as we flick through the pages of magazines, scroll through social media feeds or travel on the morning commute. Our attention is constantly being tugged at and jostled for. It's up to us to pull it back: to guard it fiercely and bestow it carefully. Attention is precious; Mary Oliver likened it to devotion.[1] Becoming aware of the quality and direction of our attention allows us to feel more present, experiencing the moments of our lives in a conscious way. Should our attention alight on something that engenders a feeling of pause or a flicker of interest or astonishment, that's when we have found a little story to tell.

Mihaly Csikszentmihalyi, Professor of Psychology and author of the classic work *Flow*, refers to attention as 'psychic energy'. He notes the difference between attention that is focused, like an intentional beam, and attention that is scattered and diffused. Our attention has innate power – it can be directed in such a way as to improve our lives, or its direction can make us unhappy.

We *create* ourselves, he explains, by the ways in which we invest our attention: 'memories, thoughts, and feelings are all shaped by how we use it'.[2] Attention is precious and it is also limited. The way in which we direct it can determine not just what we experience, but *who we are*.

Directing attention in an intentional way is a core tenet of the philosophy and practice of mindfulness. In their book, *Mindfulness* (which draws together Buddhist psychology and contemporary science) Christina Feldman and Willem Kuyken use a similar metaphor, writing that mindfulness requires 'deploying attention like a flashlight beam, *choosing* where to shine the light and what to leave in darkness'.[3] This imagery makes clear sense to me: the light of my conscious attention illuminating particular instants amongst a cloud of familiarity and oversight. We can alter our beam of attention, adjusting its width and brightness. Like the imaginary movie camera with which you focussed on the moment in Chapter One, the beam of your attention can shine on the entirety of a scene or on just the smallest detail, depending on how you direct and focus it. Attempting to consciously control the light of our attention and to shine it around our present experience can lead to a fuller understanding of what Feldman and Kuyken call 'the nuances of the moment'.[4]

In my own storytelling practice, I have found that experiencing moments in a mindful way allows me to be more mentally present, which helps me to be attentive to the little stories of my life. I do not, strictly speaking, practise mindfulness, but over time I have come to understand that some of my instinctive creative processes are similar to the techniques used in mindfulness and meditation. I am alert to the nuances of the moment and I am constantly learning to direct my attention in a way that will illuminate the stories I seek: stories of the unexpected, the forgotten, the imperfect and the transient. As one 2020 study showed,[5] mindfulness is not entirely without risk and, should you wish to begin a mindfulness practice, I would urge you to seek the guidance of a qualified mindfulness practitioner. I do believe, however, that reflecting on some principles of mindfulness can help us, as storytellers, to learn to inhabit the moment more fully. We can take inspiration from the ideas of mindfulness and meditation, allowing our creative processes to absorb some of their teachings, which can assist us as we tell our little stories.

I am never more fully in the moment than when I take an early walk with my camera in the foggy woods. Rather than dulling my senses, I find that fog sharpens them – colours appear brighter, sounds seem clearer. Familiar paths are transformed into an unfamiliar realm; when immersed in a cloud, everything feels new. On one particular September morning, the air is hazy as I walk my youngest son to school. On the hill above the town, I can see a covering of fog: a cloud resting on the treetops. I know that it won't be long before the sun burns through, so the moment I'm home, I grab my camera and hurry out of the door. Up on the hill, the air is still heavy with fog, silvery amongst the beech trees. The light is soft and diffused, intensifying the colour of the leaves; they glow green, with a sprinkling of yellow. I can hear small creatures moving at the bottom of the hedgerows – birds, or shrews, perhaps? The trees sway and rustle, and water drips from their branches. Underfoot, the first of the fallen leaves crackle; it is the day before the autumn equinox and we are in the pause between seasons. Summer is fading into autumn. Silvery spiderwebs glow in the hawthorn trees and wood pigeons coo softly.

When I walk in the foggy woods, I forget all else. My to-do list, the day ahead. All fades away as I feel the damp air on my face and watch pale light shimmer between bending branches. Fog softens the edges of everything and I never tire of its transformative power, anointing all it touches with mystery. One particularly cold, grey and densely foggy November morning a few years ago, I met

an old gentleman who was walking alone in the woods.
He smiled at me and my camera and said 'This is my
favourite time of the year – it's beautiful, isn't it?' Not
everyone sees it, but there is indeed a unique mystery to
a foggy November morning. I smiled and agreed with
him and we passed on our ways. Later, reflecting on
this brief connection, it occurred to me that I have not
always seen the beauty of the fog. Over time, I have
learned to see it and it was my camera that taught me.
Looking through the viewfinder caused me to pause;
seeking the light caused me to understand how the fog
softened it; choosing a frame for my composition caused
me to search out the details that made the scene sing. With
my camera in hand, a walk in the fog becomes a mindful
experience – a quiet and meditative start to the day.

On the other side of the field that runs alongside the
woodland, a golden glow grows stronger: the sun is
breaking through the cloud. Leaves float diagonally down
across the path, pushed by the wind. The fog, patchy now,
also drifts and swirls. Water droplets land on branches,
sparkling like jewels. My camera on my shoulder, I take
the path that leads me home, to a hot cup of tea and
my beckoning laptop. The sun has come out, the foggy
moment has passed, the morning hush is over and the
day must now begin.

A mindful approach to storytelling can bring you closer to moments
of everyday magic. Mindfulness is defined by writer and Zen
Buddhist monk Thích Nhất Hạnh as the practice of 'deeply
touching every moment of daily life'.[6] He writes that to experience
mindfulness is to 'remember that life is a wonder: we are here, and
we should live our lives deeply'.[7] He describes the importance of
noticing not just the world around us, but also the sensations of our
bodies. An unremarkable experience – such as walking on a foggy
day – can contain wonder if we alter our perception of it and try to
live it deeply. Becoming more awake to our senses and the daily

reality of our lives changes how we experience the present moment. Experiencing life in a mindful way can give an enhanced awareness of the world around us. It can also give an enhanced awareness of the world within us, creating feelings of awe and offering a stronger sense of who we are.

Being deliberately present in the moment is the way I find focus in my creative practice. Whether I am recording an experience with words or with a photograph, I direct my attention to what is happening in the here and now by engaging directly with my senses. I observe what I can hear, what I can smell, the textures that I can see and feel, the temperature of the air and the direction and quality of the light. Some of these elements are best captured in words, some in an image, and some are difficult to capture at all, but noticing them enriches my engagement with the moment. Consciously taking note of sensory impressions is a technique used in mindfulness, but it is also an important tool for storytelling. Author and story guru Bobette Buster believes that there is always one primary sense that dominates any specific memory. Tuning in to this sense memory and evoking it as you tell your story will allow you not only to reconnect with the sensations that you are describing, but also to form a connection to your story's audience, pulling them with you into the moment.[8] (You'll find a fascinating interview with Bobette in Chapter Seven, in which she generously shares her storytelling insights.)

The Here and Now

Experiment with a here-and-now exercise. This is a perfect way of consciously experience the present moment – the here and now – with all of your senses. Consider the following:

- What can you see?
- What can you hear?
- What touch sensations do you feel?
- What textures do you notice?
- What physical sensations do you feel (e.g. hunger, ache, etc.)
- What can you smell?
- What is the temperature and humidity of the air?
- What is the quality of the light?
- What additional sensations or feelings do you notice in yourself, here and now?

Record your responses in your journal.

Any moment is, by definition, brief and fleeting: one single instant in the endless sea of time – a vastness that we continuously pass through, often unthinkingly. Collecting little stories is a way to pull out individual moments from time's unstoppable tide swell. The poet Vita Sackville-West wrote of catching moments with a net, although she saw them not as fish but as fluttering butterflies. Writing was, she felt, a way in which to 'clap the net over the butterfly of the moment',[9] capturing it before it passes and is forgotten. I love this metaphor; seeing moments as bright, fragile butterflies makes perfect sense to me. Moments – like butterflies – are elusive things, often possessed of beauty and sometimes ephemeral mystery. When I find myself drawn to a butterfly moment I try to understand what makes it interesting to me. Even a familiar moment can tell me something fresh about my world if I observe it with thoughtful awareness. I want to tell the story of moments that express a feeling of yearning, that make unexpected sense, or answer a question I didn't realize I had asked – moments that encapsulate something greater than themselves. I catch butterfly moments gently, protecting their delicate wings as I observe them carefully. I make a record with words or a photograph and then accept that they must fly away, leaving me with their image to remember them by.

Writing is a tool with which to catch moments, but the process of writing can also be a mindful activity in itself. In her book *The Joy of Mindful Writing*, Joy Kenward suggests we should approach writing with an appreciation of its innate sense of space: the promising space of the empty page, the physical spaces between words and paragraphs, the imaginative space of developing ideas and the pauses for space as we consider what to write. By choosing to contemplate these spaces quietly rather than fearfully, she says that 'we can feel peaceful and adventurous at the same time'.[10] In my own writing, I find it encouraging to regard the blank page in this way – not as daunting, but as filled with possibility. I try to accept my natural pauses for thought as necessary, rather than alarming. Some writers have likened writing to meditation, a practice that

MOMENTS — LIKE BUTTERFLIES
— ARE ELUSIVE THINGS.

can be used cultivate a state of mindfulness. Natalie Goldberg, a writer who studied Zen meditation for over a decade, says in *Writing Down the Bones* that meditation and writing practice exist in harmony: 'there is no separation between writing, life and the mind'.[11] She counsels writers to begin by listening deeply to the world around them. This profound listening – a form of paying attention – is a starting point for capturing reality with words.

A meditative approach to writing can help you to tell your little stories. First, choose a journalling prompt (you'll find at least one in every chapter of this book). I would suggest beginning with a blank page in your notebook. Take a moment before you write. Consider the page in front of you as a benign space, even an inviting one. Be open to the possibilities of this space and take time to listen – to the world around you and the voice within you. Writing, like meditation, calls for the avoidance of distraction – putting aside the ever-present temptations of the internet, for example. If your mind wanders, return it gently to the page. A meditative approach to writing means accepting pauses for thought. As you wait for words to come, do you experience any feeling of stillness? Finding peace (rather than frustration or anxiousness) in the spaces between the words takes conscious application. Writing, like meditation, is an inward-looking practice that can allow us to reflect upon and express our truest selves. Both practices are considered to be most effective when they take place regularly. Julia Cameron, (author of the book and creativity course *The Artist's Way*) advocates a daily stream-of-consciousness writing exercise called 'Morning Pages'. She considers Morning Pages to be in themselves a form of meditation that can offer what she terms 'the light of insight' and help us to effect change in our lives.[12] You may wish to experiment with adopting a short daily writing practice. I find that the more consistently I sit down to write, the more likely I am to attain a peaceful state of contemplation when I do turn to a fresh page of my notebook, or open a blank document on my laptop, the cursor gently ticking.

A Window Through the Seasons

Deliberately paying attention to the changing seasons is one way in which we can learn to be aware of the nuances of the moment. The seasons' flow is a constant background to our days, and the shifts between them are gradual and subtle. For this exercise, choose a window (in your home, place of work, or somewhere that you regularly spend time). Think of the window as a picture frame, the scene beyond it an endlessly changing painting.

Take time to look out of the window. Slow down and allow yourself to get lost in the view, whatever it may be. In your journal, write a description of the scene you see through the window. Try to anchor your writing in the present moment and the current season. Without directly stating the season, which specifics can you include that indicate it? Think about weather, the sky, the strength and direction of the light, colour tones, nature's visible changes, the clothes that people are wearing and the emotions that the scene evokes in you. If you would like to, you could also record the scene with a photograph – ideally one that you can stick into your journal beside your words.

During the course of the year, repeat this exercise in your journal as often as you feel inclined to – this will allow you to really observe the subtle flow of the seasons and to immerse yourself in your particular view, directing your attention to all that you see within the window's frame. Get to know the world outside your window in spring, summer, autumn and winter, but also pay attention to your window view during the borders between seasons; observe the transition points when summer merges slowly into autumn, or winter into spring.

Like writing, photography can be a meditative activity. Maintaining focus is central to meditation and it is also central to photography – in terms of focussed attention, but also the physical act of focussing the camera on a chosen subject. Both meditation and photography lead us to rethink our understanding of the ordinary by choosing to pay intense attention to elements of the everyday. For me, photography certainly feels akin to meditation. The presence of my camera in my hand or around my neck immediately pulls me deeper into the moment, reminding me to engage anew with my surroundings, however familiar they may be. My camera becomes part of me, an invitation for me to tell the story of the now. There is always something to photograph if I open my eyes to the world. When I look through the camera's viewfinder (or the border of my phone's screen), I let go of the past and the future, thinking only of what I can see *right now* and of the most clear and meaningful way in which to capture it. The confines of the tiny frame force me to focus myself as well as the image – concentration and hands must both be unwavering. My body is still, my breath is controlled: the camera unites my hands, eyes and mind. I am utterly absorbed, rapt, fully present and intensely alive. Buddhist and teacher Stephen Bachelor suggests that this alignment of body and senses in the instant before releasing the shutter creates an intensity in the resultant image that offers us a 'glimpse into the heart of the moment'.[13]

Photography, like writing, is a tool with which to capture butterfly moments, pulling them out of time and preserving them for posterity. A camera records what exists in front of the lens, but it also records something of the photographer who stands behind it. In a sense, every photograph is a self-portrait, offering a glimpse into the mind and feelings of the photographer who framed it. We leave indelible emotional fingerprints on every image that we compose. Capturing a meditative moment with a camera allows us to return to that same moment in the future. Photographs are passports with which we can travel back to re-experience the precise minute that an image was taken. We are reminded of the specific reality that we experienced in the seconds before the shutter clicked and – should

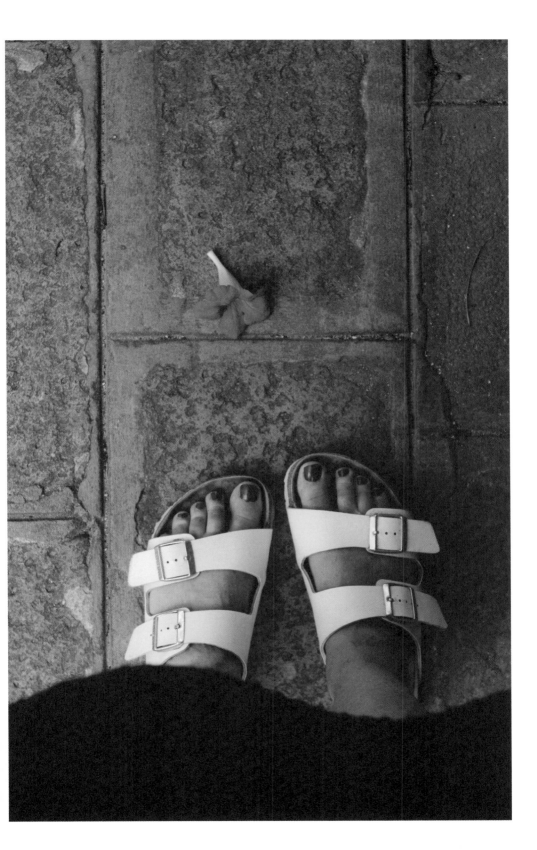

we wish to – we can revisit it over and over again. For me, this is an important reason to ensure that I regularly print my digital images. I will never tire of the joy that a packet of photographs brings. Holding an actual moment in my hand (before framing it, sliding it between the pages of a book or sticking it to the wall above my desk) is the closest thing to witchcraft that I know.

Photographer Dorothea Lange said that 'the camera is an instrument that teaches people how to see without a camera'.[14] There is no doubt in my mind that, over the years, the practice of taking daily photographs has begun to teach me to view the world in a different way. Photography encourages us not just to look, but to actively see. When we look, we direct our gaze in a specific direction, but when we see, we perceive, imagine, recognize and understand. Choosing to pay close attention to the present moment and learning to maintain steady focus is the starting point for a photography practice that continues to develop our ability to see, until eventually this altered perception becomes a part of who we are. I now find that even when I am without my camera, in my mind I still compose an image when I notice a detail that tells me a story. Learning to see is one benefit of choosing to fully enter into moments. It requires us to engage not just with our eyes, but also with our imaginations. For me, meditative photography is less about training my photographic eye and more about teaching myself to be conscious of how I feel as I compose an image, considering how I can communicate that feeling with my camera and deciding what stories I am trying to tell. It is about learning to take pictures not with my camera but with my heart.

Photography – like mindfulness – is an exercise in wonder. With my camera in hand, I look for the curious, the remarkable, or the unfamiliar. I am actively seeking amazement – the thrill that I experience when I realize that the light is *just right*, notice an intricate shadow pattern, come across a perfect fallen bloom or discover an elegantly weathered facade. These are some of the scenes that make my own heart beat faster, but wonder touches each of us differently. The physical act of wandering can allow us to experience wonder – taking an aimless stroll with my camera and no fixed destination in mind, is my favourite way to spend an hour or two. It always leaves me feeling refreshed and inspired. Walking is not just a source of storytelling inspiration, in itself it can also be a kind of mindfulness, which Thích Nhất Hạnh calls 'walking meditation'. He explains that this means to 'arrive in the present moment with every step'.[15] Both photography and mindfulness call for us to be alert to the sensations of the moment as we walk. In this way we open ourselves up to the possibility of wonder.

Mindfulness emphasizes the importance of being actively present, of seeking to know and understand moments just as they are. But although mindfulness techniques can develop our ability to experience moments more deeply (helping us to capture and tell better stories), storytelling differs from mindfulness because it is not merely a present moment activity. We exist in the present and, with practice, we can learn to pay close attention to the experiences of the current moment, but storytelling also requires us to cultivate an awareness of the relationship between moments. The present will soon be the past and our aim is to capture something of it, as a memento for ourselves in the future. We don't just *live* the moment, we also reflect on it and record it with words and images so that we will be able to recall it. Storytellers weave an overarching narrative that connects moment with moment and story with story. We make connections between events and experiences, feelings and ideas. Thought and memory are where we storytellers feel at home.

The physical act of writing something down means that we are more likely to remember it, and the same can be true of photography – I find that the time that I take in framing and composing an image can leave an impression not just on the camera's memory card, but also in my own memory. More often, however, moments pass and are lost to me, only returning to my mind when I find a stray photograph at the bottom of a box, or flick through the pages of an old notebook. Words and photographs are imperfect mediums for preserving moments, but they are the best that we have. Photographer Aaron Siskind said that photography 'remembers little things, long after you have forgotten everything' and I would suggest that the same is true of writing. I want to be alert to the nuances of the moment and to observe little things, but for me, noticing alone is not enough. The impulse to gather my stories – to collect and record moments, like a magpie drawn to gather glittering treasures – is an intrinsic part of who I am.

I tell stories of moments that I wish to remember, but as I do so, I recognize there will be numerous moments that I will forget. I have tried to make peace with the inevitability of these forgotten moments, which writer Sarah Manguso describes as 'the price of continued participation in life, a force indifferent to time'.[16] It is, of course, impossible for anyone to collate every single moment, but I choose to pay attention (seeking wonder and capturing it) as best I can. Time continues apace and, however many little stories I tell, my record of life will be an imperfect one – my butterfly collection will be incomplete. I know this. We are here in the moments that we remember, but we are also here in the moments that we forget.

A Mindful Photowalk

Photowalk simply means taking a walk and recording it with photographs: for this exercise, I'd like you to take your camera on a walk. A simple camera is the best choice for a photowalk because it allows you to focus on framing what you see, rather than becoming distracted by camera settings. For this reason, I'd suggest using your phone or, if you have one, an instant camera.

What's important is not *where* you walk, but *how* you walk. If you choose a familiar route, allow yourself to experience the walk in this particular season and with this specific light. As you walk, use your camera to record changes that you notice, or details that draw your eye on this particular day. Alternatively, you may choose to make new discoveries by walking somewhere that you've never been before. Wherever you walk, try to still your mind and focus on the sensations of the moment, observing the details that you pass. Remember not just to look, but to consciously see. Take pictures of whatever calls to you – record what it is that means something to you.

When you want to record something with a photograph, take time to pause and ground yourself. Take a breath. Try to filter out any distractions around you and concentrate only on what you see in the frame. Experiment with reframing your subject – moving closer, or further away, higher up, or lower down – until you have a composition that best tells the story of what your eye was drawn to. You should photograph whatever is of interest to you in the moment, but if you need inspiration, you may wish to consider some of the following themes:

- Signs that someone has passed by
- Looking up
- Looking down
- Textures
- Decay
- Light patterns
- Growth
- The unexpected

Looking
Inwards

Our stories begin with ourselves.

As storytellers, we pay attention to the world outside – observing closely, listening carefully, recording faithfully – but to tell our own stories we also look inwards. In her essay *On Keeping a Notebook*, Joan Didion wrote that by keeping a notebook she was seeking to *'remember what it was to be me*: that is always the point'.[1] I have her words pinned above my desk: *remember what it was to be me.* They speak to the heart of why, a natural chronicler, I've always kept notebooks, collaged photographs, jotted down stories. How do I feel in this moment? Who *am I* in this moment? What does it mean, right now, to be me? We write things down – memories, snippets, thoughts, observations – in order to connect with our ever-changing selves, to record who we are in the instant. In our notebooks, we press our past selves between the pages like diaphanous flowers, so that we can look back and remember who we used to be.

Photographs, particularly self-portraits, can be used in the same way. For example, a holiday selfie, smiling sun-tanned face in front of a gorgeous view or at the summit of a recently climbed peak, is guided by the impulse to remember; the desire to preserve the place, the experience and, most importantly, the feeling. This is where I am right now, this is *who* I am. We record little stories to remember who we are, who we were, who we want to be. We seek to capture our fleeting emotions, the impressions and sensory experiences of a specific instant. We want to be able to recall who we are in a given moment.

*I*t was in order to remember how it feels to be me that I developed a habit of snapping a self-portrait whenever I swim in the sea. A love of outdoor swimming is in my blood; I come from a big family of hardy individuals with a penchant for seeking out, and diving into, bodies of cold water. My beloved grandad was the original swimmer; he swam in the sea year-round and in 1969 was one of the founding members of his local Christmas Day swim. As a child, and even a young woman, the appeal of cold-water swimming was lost on me. I spent many family Christmases huddled on the beach, watching braver family members dash with him into the bitter waves. I often swam with my Grandad in the summertime – an empty early morning beach, the sea a clear, glassy pond – but I didn't brave a winter swim until after he was gone, when I was grown up, with children of my own.

The day after his funeral was the first day of December, a sparkling morning. At my cousin Jasmine's suggestion, we assembled on the beach to remember him by sharing together in the thing he loved: his five children, over a dozen grandchildren and other assorted members of the family. My Grandma watched, holding a flask of scalding coffee laced with brandy, as we lined up along the sand in our swimming costumes, hopping, rubbing our arms and squealing in the icy air. My uncle counted down and we dashed together, splashing and laughing, into the sea. The shock gripped my chest, squeezing the breath out of me as the cold water pulled me close. I swam a few strokes towards the glittering sun. My skin tingled with *an exhilaration close to pain. Grief and loss were interwoven with joy and gratitude, to be alive, to be with the people that I love – sharing in a wild requiem.*

Since that day, I have sought the chill waves at every opportunity, craving the sense of being truly, consciously alive. I have taught myself to swim year-round, chasing the sensation that my cousin Molly (who often swims with me) calls 'the zing'. When I emerge from the water, the tingling numbness in my limbs turning to exhilaration, I snap a quick picture on my phone: my head and shoulders, with the sea behind me. I am usually bedraggled; my mascara is slightly smudged, my hair wind-whipped, but that doesn't matter. These photographs are for no-one else: I take them to remember what it is to be me, with the salt clinging to my skin and my toes still submerged in the water. On days when I feel frustrated, trapped or uninspired, I think back to the sea and the memory of the shock of the waves. I sustain myself by scrolling back through my camera roll to these saltwater selfies, reminded of the freedom I felt and that I will, one day soon, feel again.

THIS IS WHERE I AM RIGHT NOW,
THIS IS *WHO* I AM.

Using Photographs to Remember the People We Used to Be

Find a photograph from your past, one that both captures a moment and encapsulates a feeling. It could be from a couple of months ago, or from many years ago. It may be an image of you, or an image that you composed and shot. Whether you were behind the lens or in front of it, choose an image that reminds you what it was to be you in the instant that the camera shutter clicked. Look carefully. Reconsider. Where were you in that moment? Who were you in that moment? How did it feel to be you at that time? How do you feel now, looking back on it?

What is there about this image that you could re-create in order to compose a photograph that captures the current moment?

Collected together, the memories and moments that you choose to record build a picture of what speaks to your heart. Looking back at them can allow you to reconsider events, giving you an understanding of what truly matters to you and a clearer sense of your own intentions. Flicking through the pages of your journal or scrolling through a collection of your pictures, you find yourself reflected there, not just in your self-portraits, but in each snippet of writing and every image that you have taken. The unifying factor is always you – your eye composes the pictures, your hand notes down the words.

Journalling is the way in which I record and compile the stories of my life, but my interpretation of the concept of journalling is expansive. For me, it's a process that can take many forms: scrawling in notebooks, keeping a diary, compiling images and keepsakes in a scrapbook, sharing online through a blog or micro-blogging platform such as Instagram. Keeping a journal, in whatever form, is about being true to yourself: a journal is a form of self-expression. Tristine Rainer, an expert on diary, journal and memoir writing, advises journal writers to 'write fast, write everything, include everything, write from your feelings, write from your body, accept whatever comes'.[2]

In the same way that having a conscious awareness of your feelings prior to taking a photograph can intensify your engagement with the moment, taking time to look inwards and write from your feelings as you record stories in your journal will give your writing greater resonance. This technique can also be helpful when recounting a little story for an audience; for example, in a social media caption, if you write from *your* feelings, your story will almost certainly connect with the feelings of your audience.

I once shared on Instagram a photograph of a pretty thatched cottage, with the caption:

When I was a little girl, my Dad was a thatcher. He knew how to weave straw – not into gold – but into a roof, which I always found just as magical. I used to love visiting him at work and finding him perched up on the ridge of a house, a tall ladder-climb away. Thatched cottages like this beauty will always remind me of those days, standing in my yellow raincoat, gazing up at my Daddy who could touch the sky.

The image itself was simple, a picturesque cottage quickly snapped on my iPhone whilst passing through a small Welsh village. I was taken aback by the large volume of positive responses that it received. Although the cottage was charming, I realized that what had spoken to people was the recollection it had sparked for me. I had told a little story that recalled my childhood feelings of love for my father and my awe at what he could do. It was those feelings that connected with my audience and drew them, for just a moment, into my world.

Looking inwards and tuning in to your feelings is a powerful storytelling technique. When you pick up your camera to take a photograph, take a moment to reflect on how you feel in this instant. A camera is just a *tool*; the picture comes from you, created by the connection between your eye and your heart. How you feel will inform what you see and what you choose to capture. If you are feeling melancholy, for example, you may see the appeal of quiet, poignant scenes – such as fallen petals on the pavement or an empty coffee cup – or if you are feeling joyful, the sparkle of sunshine on the water may call to you. The emotion that you feel when you compose an image will contribute to its visual mood, whether it's joyful, celebratory, sad, pensive or thoughtful. There are a number of elements that combine to create the mood of an image – subject matter, colour palette, light, viewpoint and weather conditions all have a part to play and having a conscious awareness of these elements is a key part of composing storytelling images. When I take a photograph that I love, what matters to me is less that it *looks* right, and more that it *feels* right. The same is true of written stories. Becoming more aware of ourselves and of who we are in a given moment allows us to channel this awareness into our journalling.

Being aware of the natural flow of your feelings is a pivotal step towards developing an authentic storytelling process and – in time – a unique storytelling voice. It can, however, also be helpful to experiment with a process that offers a little more guidance: a journalling technique that teaches you to utilize your emotions in a conscious, managed way. This technique is called positive journalling, and it involves deliberately channelling positive emotions and engaging with them when writing. A popular example of this is the keeping of a gratitude journal, a technique that I've often used in my own journalling practice, particularly in the winter months when positivity can feel more elusive to me!

Practising gratitude has well-documented benefits: a 2018 white paper on the Science of Gratitude from University of California, Berkeley reported that 'gratitude practices, like keeping a "gratitude journal" or writing a letter of gratitude can increase people's happiness and overall mood'.[3] A gratitude practice has been associated with improved well-being: one study found that experiencing daily feelings of gratitude led to a range of positive feelings of well-being.[4] At its simplest, gratitude journalling is the action of reflecting on and noting in your journal things that you are grateful for. This could be a person, an object, a place, a memory: anything that inspires gratitude. There are different ways to approach it but making a short daily list of five to ten things that you are grateful for is often suggested as a good starting point. I find that reflecting on gratitude, even as an occasional practice, helps me to develop the habit of considering my life thoughtfully and of paying attention to – and remembering to be grateful for – its details. By taking time to note down what I feel grateful for, I remind myself of what I love and my sense of love expands to encompass not just the great and important, but also the tiny and seemingly insignificant. Recording little stories from your life can in itself be viewed as a type of gratitude practice; by recognizing a moment – however small – as being worthy of memory, you touch it with love.

An excellent example of a collection of stories focused through the lens of one particular emotion is *The Book of Delights*, Ross Gay's book of essays based on the premise of writing a daily essay about something delightful. He made the commitment to 'spend time thinking and writing about delight every day',[5] and the resultant essays (each offering the reader a little story) are luminous with truth. A song, a bird, a movie title, a Latin phrase, a scrap of graffiti, a man in a café with an umbrella – every delight inspires a short essay that he develops in an often unexpected (and not always purely delightful) direction from its starting point. Looking at the world through the lens of delight could be saccharine: Ross Gay makes it anything but. He demonstrates that delight is part of a full emotional range which includes sorrow, frustration, anger and pain. Positive emotions (such as delight) can be celebrated without ignoring more difficult emotions. I am interested in the idea that if we choose to channel positive emotions in our storytelling, we can do so in a way that remains an authentic expression of our full lived experience. Delight doesn't push aside emotions such as sorrow or fear, it exists alongside them. We can embrace positive emotions without losing touch with the complexity of ourselves.

An intentional journalling discipline, such as a gratitude journal or delight-writing, is one way to create a record of often-overlooked moments of small joys. It develops the skill of close observation. Making the choice to consciously seek out delight (or joy, or any other positive emotion) in our storytelling can lead to us experiencing more of it. Ross Gay writes that through the practice of recording a daily delight, he developed his 'delight muscle', explaining that 'the more you study delight, the more delight there is to study'.[6]

Journalling with Emotion

In your journal, experiment with writing from the perspective of a specific emotion. Begin by selecting a positive sentiment (gratitude, delight, happiness, etc.) and focus on seeing and recording the world through the lens of this particular emotion. Use the following prompts to help you to do so:

- As you move through your day, when you experience the positive emotion you have chosen, tune in to your senses and take note of what you can see, hear, touch, taste and smell. Record this sense experience, in as much detail as possible, in your journal. Can you use your sense observations to tell the little story of this moment?

- Locate a physical object which causes you to feel the positive emotion that you have chosen. For example, a smooth pebble given to you by someone you care about may represent happiness to you. Record this object with a photograph (if you can, print it out and stick it in your journal) and write the story of what it means to you.

- Remember a time in the past when you experienced the positive emotion that you have chosen. In your journal, tell the story of this experience.

- How can you draw more of the positive emotion that you have chosen into your life? How does it connect to your intentions and dreams? Write about this in your journal.

- Commit to thinking and writing about this positive emotion daily and adhere to this for at least one week. At the end of the week, consider if your feelings or your writing have altered in any way. Are you beginning to develop a stronger sense of this emotion? You may wish to continue the practice for longer.

When you have completed one or more of the prompts, why not repeat them using a different positive emotion as your stimulus, or extend your daily practice beyond a week, incorporating it into your journal writing and storytelling.

In his book, Ross Gay refers to 'TEMPORAL ALLEGIANCE'[7] (a phase he presents in capital letters and writes on his hand to remind himself). I was drawn to this concept which means, I think, being loyal to – paying attention to – transitory experiences that exist in the present moment. It implies an awareness of time, complex unstoppable time, and it echoes my own preoccupations with what it means to live fully in, and to capture, a moment. Noticing delightful moments allows us to live them more deeply. Recording is our attempt to capture them (a word which is curiously sometimes used as a noun when describing a photograph: 'nice capture'.) All our photographs (all our little stories) are attempts to capture a moment and to pause time, just for an instant.

In her book *Ongoingness: The End of a Diary*, writer Sarah Manguso is deeply preoccupied with time. She recognizes 'the bracing speed of the one-way journey that guides human experience'.[8] Her extensive diary writing begins as a defence against missed moments, but during the course of the book, particularly following the birth of her son, her experience of time is altered. She begins to accept the unstoppable pace of life and the inevitability of moments being forgotten. No one can hope to recall – or to record – everything. Still, practising dailiness and making a conscious choice to transcribe selected moments gives us the chance not just to record events, but to transform them. 'The experience is no longer experience', says Manguso: 'It is writing.'[9] Although we cannot stop time, we can transmute it: into writing, into pictures. We can turn it into stories.

Seeking out the invisible or unappreciated parts of life involves cultivating the skill of noticing. How do you feel? What do your senses tell you? What is it that invites your gaze? What are the things that *only you* pay attention to? Like a 'delight muscle', developing the skill of noticing takes time and practice. I have found that learning to look closely, and being open to the world, has allowed me to appreciate the wonder that comes from finding beauty in the banal, an experience that Jessica Backhaus (a German photographer known for her passion for capturing beauty in the ordinary) describes as being like glimpsing a shooting star.[10] The beauty that we find will be different for each of us: you record the world, and the things that *you* care about, from your own particular viewpoint. The delights (or joys, or things you are grateful for) that you discover will be particular to you. The little stories that have the most meaning are the ones that belong to you alone. Take pleasure in knowing that no-one views the world in quite same way. Noticing is about slowing down and observing carefully. What do you see when you study closely and then study again? You look around you, but you are also looking inwards, tuning in to your intuition, your daydreams, your moods and your thoughts.

There was a time when I felt that my own daily life was far too mundane and ordinary to contain any stories worth telling. I was a sleep-deprived new mother, with a baby and a toddler – my days felt like a hazy cycle of nappies and milk. Routines seemed stultifying and I was lost, believing myself to have nothing whatsoever of interest to say. Then, in my spare minutes – during naptimes, or late at night – I began to find corners of the internet that women had claimed for their own, where they were capturing their lives with words and pictures. This gave me the impetus to look more closely at my own everyday life and I learned to see the world afresh. I picked up my camera for the first time in years and tentatively began to take note of what I was drawn to, thus beginning a creative journey that in time led me back to myself. I came to understand that what makes for interesting stories is not drama and action, but attentiveness and quality of observation. All our lives are full of little stories, and we each have a singular and remarkable point of view. Before we can *tell* our stories, we must first teach ourselves to observe them.

If you are accustomed to always telling stories that appeal to others (e.g. by sharing on social media), can you give yourself grace to write down some of your little stories privately, in a journal that is just for you? Although a journal can become an excellent source of ideas for stories to tell online, in itself it is a private undertaking. An act of creation for you alone. A communication with yourself, motivated not by external approval but by exploration and creativity. Observing and recording what you love – what brings you delight or joy– can lead you in unexpected directions. You may find that the practice expands what makes you happy, allowing you to find appreciation for unexpected elements of your life. It can develop your understanding of who you are, strengthening your sense of who you are.

Preserving your little stories is an act of self-reflection, a cultivation of your inner self. This is your life and telling your stories can help you to see it, and yourself, more clearly. Looking closely at the world and documenting your responses to it can allow you to perceive your experiences with greater comprehension, leading to enhanced self-awareness. In recording your stories – whether with words or with photographs – you also capture yourself. I believe that through recording the stories of my life, I can discover and record the unique story of myself. Your story, like mine, cannot be repeated by someone else because it is singular and special – you are singular and special – and this uniqueness is something to be celebrated. Looking thoughtfully inwards helps you to understand more about who you are and what you have to say; the stories that only you can tell. By recognizing your particular combination of interests, preoccupations, abilities and characteristics, you can begin to draw on the deep source of creativity that comes from your inner self.

As you widen the scope of your daily perception, noticing the previously unseen, feeling grateful for what was once unappreciated and reflecting on how you feel and what you notice, you may find that patterns emerge. Do your personal preoccupations bring to mind specific themes? Over many years of telling my own little stories, I have come to realize that I am fascinated by the passage of time. So much of what I am repeatedly drawn to is indicative

of it: the turning of the seasons; decaying old buildings; the colour tones of analogue photographs; my reflection in the mirror; the changing faces of my children; fossils, sea glass, hagstones. Discovering what it is that you personally are drawn to can help you tune in more closely to your deeper interests, developing sources of inspiration for your storytelling and creative practice.

As you gather inspiration from the world around you, you can balance this with an inward-looking search for meaning. In my own creative process, I take an introspective approach; I have begun to ask myself the question 'why'. Why was my eye drawn to this plant, bejewelled with raindrops, that grows from a crack in the pavement? What does this tell me about who I am? How can I tell this particular little story and in what way is this a part of my wider story? I am developing my understanding of what it is that inspires me, the reasons for this and the patterns that emerge. The plant bejewelled by raindrops drew my eye with its sparkle – a flash of reflective light against a dull grey pavement. I noticed it because I am always searching for the light and have trained my eye to see it, but also because, to me, the weeds that break through the concrete represent a kind of hope, and on this particular rainy day, hope was something that I needed.

Let me share with you some common sources of inspiration that I use to tell my little stories, with suggestions for how you might use them to tell your own. Begin your search for inspiration by looking outwards, discover what you are drawn to and the stories that it prompts you to record, but remember to take your creative process one step further – look inwards and ask yourself *why*. Bring yourself back to this question: how does the little story that you have chosen to tell relate to your own unique story of self – the *story of who you are?*

HOME

My home is probably very different from your home; each is as
unique as we are and they are usually the places where we feel
most completely ourselves. My house is old (turn-of-the-century
– over a hundred years) almost always cold, dustier than it should
be and – thanks to my three lively young sons – it's unfailingly
messy too. There are scattered toys, precarious stacks of books,
baskets of shoes and discarded clothes. I don't love the mess, but
I've accepted it, invariably choosing to write rather than to tidy. At
home, I gather inspiration in small, specific corners. In my tiny attic
office, I keep a collection of photographs stuck to the wall beside
my desk, reminders of what it was to be me at different points in
my life. The hooks on my office wall are where I hang pickings from
my walks: a wreath of drying Russian vine, or a bundle of tiny larch
cones. I love, as I told you, my kitchen table and the objects that
accumulate there through the course of the day. My wooden stairs
are scruffy – fading white paint along the edges, scuff marks, divots
– but they are a spot in which I often sit, to think, read, or take a
photograph. Like the cracked tiles in the hall, they remind me that
other people lived in this house before me and that their stories are
part of the fabric of the building, as one day mine will be too.

It can seem, from a glance at social media, that homes should be
more aspirational than inspirational, but being immaculate does not
make a room interesting. I spent a couple of years as deputy editor
for a creative interiors magazine, and what I always found most
compelling about any home were the personal stories behind the
objects in the images we published: treasures from flea markets,
souvenirs from travels, shells collected from beaches, photographs
of beloved people, furniture or fabrics handed down from family
members. There are almost certainly items in your home that you
see so often you have almost ceased to notice them, and yet those
items are ripe with stories. Choose one, an object in your home that
is special to you and write down its story, writing from the heart and
accepting whatever comes. Take out your camera and snap some

still-life scenes; look for homely vignettes such as a pile of books on a windowsill, a shoe discarded in a doorway or a bowl of ripe strawberries. These transient – often accidental – arrangements tell stories of family, of heart and of home. Examine the feelings that these scenes provoke and try to capture this emotion in your image.

THE NATURAL WORLD

Nature is a constant source of inspiration to me, from the cowrie shells smaller than my fingernail that I found in a North Devon cove, to the vast expanses of endlessly changing sky above the flat Suffolk landscapes of my childhood. Being out in nature always restores and inspires me, particularly in the spaces that I return to time and again. I love the beech woods, the rolling fields, the hidden footpaths and the Iron Age settlements that rest beneath the surface of the land. Nothing clarifies my thoughts like a walk – or a run – through the woods. Being in open, outdoor spaces helps my ideas to flow, but it's specific natural details that inspire me. I look for the wispy spirals of *Clematis vitalba* seeds (also known as 'traveller's joy' or, less elegantly but more descriptively, 'old man's beard'). I know the places where the bluebells grow and where patches of sweet-scented wild chamomile can be found. I walk alongside the just-ploughed field that is rich with fossils. I seek out plump blackberries with their finger-staining juices.

The natural world varies according to the seasons and where you are in the world, but it is always rich with inspiration. Whatever corner of nature you have access to, whether it's a park, a field, a beach, a wood or even a window box, look closely. Observe the colours, the textures and the details. Search for treasure: an acorn, a perfect leaf, a tiny flower. Use your camera to tell the story of this place, on this day – the colours that stand out, the textures that invite the eye, the sky above and the ground below. Look carefully at what you see in front of you and consider how you feel in this moment? Write the story of what you see in front of you, or be reminded of a time in the past and write a previously untold story.

URBAN LANDSCAPE

Although I now live in a small rural town, I spent fifteen years living in a city. My feet were more accustomed to shiny rain-glistened pavements than muddy woodland paths. At weekends, I walked from one side of the city to the other down unfamiliar streets, discovering new corners – a tempting pub, a disused warehouse, a bridge across the river, a curious nose-shaped sculpture on the side of a house. As evening fell, I stopped in the park to look at the twinkling city spread out below me. I was comforted by the window-glow – the tantalizing hints of lives being lived all around me. I wheeled my son's pram (baby carriage) round and round the ruined Victorian cemetery at the edge of the city, where vines and brambles pushed up through the neglected graves, the angels wreathed with weeds. I felt drawn to the beautiful melancholy of a place thick with forgotten stories.

Cities are dynamic spaces. There is always something fresh to see, somewhere different to go, someone new to meet. The urban landscape is in a constant state of flux. Buildings don't need visible layers of peeling paint to contain layers of stories. The ever-changing streets are filled with them. In the city, look below the surface and write the stories that you find there, the stories of what the urban landscape means to you. Get to know the city through strolling. Explore hidden corners and search out little stories at the heart of your city. As you walk, have your camera to hand in order to capture the textures, the oddities and the unexpected delights that the city offers up.

SEASONS

As time passes, I find myself increasingly aware of the turning of the seasons. I mean this in terms of the speed with which the years tick by, but also in terms of the effect that seasonal changes have on the way I move through my days. Spring gives me hope, with its promise of change and new life. Spring is vibrant: a pure, deep, glowing green. Spring is baskets of starburst white wild garlic

90

flowers and the chattering of birdsong. Summer is the season that I long for and which always slips by too fast. Summer is languorous and carefree, beach days and wildflower meadows and stepping out the door with bare arms and empty pockets. Summer is ox-eye daisies and barley swaying in the breeze. Autumn is change, both endings and new beginnings. Autumn means back-to-school, piles of crunchy leaves and misty mornings. Autumn is glorious, golden, sparkling light. Winter I find quiet and calm, a time for hibernation and rest. Winter is lowering rainclouds and drifts of fresh snow. Winter is darkness and a dying-back, with a sprinkling of seasonal sparkle to carry us through.

The flow of the seasons affects the weather, the landscape and the prevailing mood. Every change of season brings with it fresh inspiration. Learning how to tell the story of a season is a never-ending process because every season is different, varying from year to year. No two summers are every exactly the same and the challenge is always to tell the story of the season that you are in right now. Be specific. Write about the weather, the tones, the temperature, the way the sunlight or the raindrops fall. Consider the changes that the season brings to your world. Make your feelings a part of the story. Use your camera to capture your mood and your experience of this specific season: look at the colour palette and the quality of light. Open yourself up to pathetic fallacy. (This is a literary term for when we see emotions in nature, for example, sadness in raindrops or confusion in fog.)

Wherever we find our inspiration, we are always reaching for the stories within ourselves. Storytelling is a tool with which to communicate with others but it is also a way to commune with yourself, to understand with greater clarity the unique self that is you. As you study the world around you, as you search for joy or delight, keep listening out for your inner voice, the voice that whispers *remember what it is to be me.*

An Inspiration Vision Board

To create an inspiration vision board, you will need: a large sheet of paper or a blank double spread of your journal, 5–10 magazines, scissors and glue. Alternatively, you could use visual search engine Pinterest (www.pinterest.com). The process of creating a vision board is a simple one. You collect together images (and, if you like, words or phrases) that inspire you, cut them out and collage them together.

Vision boards can be used in different ways, but for this vision board, the aim is to gain a better understanding of what inspires you. Try to make your selections as intuitively as you can. Flick through the magazines (or scroll through Pinterest) and tear out pictures and words or phrases that you feel drawn to, or that speak to you. Do this fairly quickly, without too much deliberation. It will take about a quarter of an hour. Once you have a pile of inspiration, go through more carefully, this time with scissors, and cut out the images that called to you. Use the glue to collage together these images in whatever way feels most appealing. If you are using Pinterest, pin all the images to a board named Inspiration Vision Board (you might choose to make this a private board).

Once you have completed your vision board, take some time to reflect on the following questions (you may wish to jot the answers down in your journal).

- Looking at your vision board, do you notice any themes?

- How do the images that you've selected make you feel?

- Are the elements that you have gathered together already present in your life, or are they things that you feel drawn to in the future?

- If you haven't included words in your vision board, can you think of three words to describe the board that you have created?

- Is there a story (or stories) that your vision board reveals about you? Is this a story that you could tell, or expand upon?

The Mystery of Creativity

Our inner voice tends to be timorous and quiet.

So it's not always easy to tune in to the soft whisper of our feelings, dreams and hopes when the clamour of the external world is an endless distraction. One way in which to direct our focus inwards is by embracing the mysterious force that is creativity. Engaging with your own creativity can help you to gain a closer understanding of who you really are. Psychologist Ellen J. Langer suggests that pursuing a creative endeavour (such as photography or writing) is a method by which you can strengthen a connection to your own inner voice and develop a clearer sense of your true self. She calls this process of creative self-discovery 'the journey home'.[1]

Our storytelling tools – photography and writing – are creative pursuits and creativity is undoubtedly an important aspect of storytelling. Indeed, it is an important element of life itself, a concept that is both familiar (we have been creating, in one form or another, since we were the youngest of children) and yet also unknowable, it remains shrouded in myth and mystery. So, what *is* creativity? Biologist E.O. Wilson, in his book *The Origins of Creativity*, considers it to be 'the unique and defining trait of our species' – describing it as 'the innate quest for originality'. Our natural human fascination with the new means that we are constantly seeking and developing that which is fresh and different, whether it's ideas, objects, processes, challenges, information, interactions or entire worlds. He suggests that we, as humans, judge our creativity according to 'the magnitude of the emotional response it evokes'.[2] The more powerful a piece of creative work is, the greater our emotional response will be. In this sense, creativity is a way to connect, not only with our inner selves, but also with those around us. Creativity – our own and that of others – teaches us to *feel*.

Human creativity is a process of endless discovery and exploration: an ongoing expressive quest. We understand creativity to be messy in the *physical* sense – the artist's paint-splattered smock, the writer's ink-stained desk or the potter with clay beneath their fingernails – but psychologist Scott Barry Kaufman and science writer Carolyn Gregoire explain that creativity is also *neurologically* messy. Creativity is multifaceted – it does not represent one single characteristic, but a complex system of characteristics. The creative process draws on the entire brain. We, as humans, are intrinsically messy; our hearts and minds are complicated and often not guided by rules or even logic. The nature of creativity reflects the disorder and complexity that are inherent in human nature; part of creativity's mystery is that it works in often paradoxical and unexpected ways. Kaufman and Gregoire highlight that creativity requires us to find a balance between such contradictions as solitude and collaboration or play and seriousness – contradictions that they suggest can be reconciled through the creative process. The benefits of our creative endeavours are greatest when we focus on this *process* – rather than the end result – for example, taking pleasure in the soothing rhythms of knitting a scarf means enjoying and engaging with the act of creation, instead of seeing it as simply a means to a warm neck. When we take enjoyment and satisfaction from the creative act itself (not just the end product), we may experience increased creative potential and intrinsic motivation.3

In storytelling terms, this means that we benefit from allowing ourselves to explore and take pleasure in the creative process of recording our experiences through writing or photography. We can embrace the inherent messiness of this process, rather than fixating on the end product of a neat journal or a beautifully curated Instagram feed. Our journals – like our lives, hearts and minds – can and should be messy. We should not feel afraid to record sad, negative or imperfect moments and we should accept the imperfections of the creative process itself. We are free to experiment, whilst accepting that we will inevitably create mess and maybe make mistakes. I have found that my own creative mistakes (however frustrating they may feel at the time) have often led to learning, developing and exploring in unexpected directions. Life is there in the crossed-out lines of writing, the scribbles in the margins and the mis-framed or out-of-focus images – life, and truth too. In this age of digital photography, we are able to immediately delete images that we feel are not quite right, an ability which can lead us on a vain search for perfection. I have found shooting on film to be a photographic process that has far more capacity for truth – for mistakes and also for unexpected successes. On many occasions, I've discovered that the image I loved most from a pack of recently developed film photographs was the least perfect one: the out-of-focus picture that changes the way I look at a scene; the accidental double-exposure; or the light leak that unexpectedly captures the dreaminess of a moment. These rare, messy, imperfect images mean far more to me than the thousands of perfectly focused shots on my iPhone camera roll; flawed, analogue beauty is what I crave. I am inspired by it and I find myself constantly trying to recall and re-create it.

Mistakes are an important part of the creative process and so too is the inner resistance that we inevitably come up against when our endeavours feel problematic. Writer Elizabeth Gilbert, author of *Big Magic: Creative Living Beyond Fear*, suggests instances when the creative act becomes a struggle – the moments that we are unsure, or our creative work feels too difficult – are actually the most important ones of all. She considers this struggle to be 'the good part, the wild part, the transformative part'[4], which – if we push through it – leads us to new revelations and an enhanced understanding of our sense of self. Gilbert writes of creativity as being 'the relationship between a human being and the mysteries of inspiration', with creativity as 'a force of enchantment'.[5] In her 2009 TED Talk 'Your Elusive Creative Genius' she notes that the idea of inspiration as a force external to us as humans dates back to the Ancient Greeks and Romans, who believed that it arrived in the form of a visiting spirit – like a guardian angel – that the Greeks called a 'daemon', and the Romans a 'genius'.[6] If creative inspiration is an external force (that we can welcome, but not influence), it comes to us as a blessing, rather than as the result of a gruelling inner struggle. Suffering and unhappiness are not necessary (or even desirable) conditions for creativity. In fact, quite the opposite – creativity can prove to be a distraction from life's troubles, a source of pleasure and fulfilment.

Nowadays, we may not all believe in visitations from a beneficent spirit, but nevertheless, creativity does retain a sense of unpredictable mystery. Personally, when I find myself in a state of creative inspiration (whether it's in the woods, with my camera in hand, or writing at the desk in my little loft-room office), I enter a kind of trance, losing track of time, forgetting to eat, becoming completely unaware of what's around me as I relinquish control and allow my ideas to guide me. This state of creative inspiration is an example of Mihaly Csikszentmihalyi's concept of *flow*. When our attention flows effortlessly, we enter this state of deep, intense concentration. During *flow*, 'thoughts, intentions, feelings, and all the senses are focussed on the same goal'.[7] As a result we may experience a 'sense of discovery' or a 'creative feeling' of being

WE SHOULD ACCEPT THE IMPERFECTIONS
OF THE CREATIVE PROCESS ITSELF.

transported to a different reality. He explains that this state of *flow*, when we achieve it, can actually have a beneficial effect on our very self; as a result of experiencing flow, a person becomes 'more of a unique individual, less predictable, possessed of rarer skills'.[8] *Flow* is not only a satisfying, enjoyable state, it also has wider benefits. Virginia Woolf once wrote in her diary (describing her writing process at that particular time): 'the well is full, ideas are rising [...] Odd how the creative power at once brings the whole universe to order'.[9] When we feel inspired – when we attain a state of creative flow – everything else fades away and all seems right with the world.

Creativity is an essential part of who we are, an innate element of ourselves that we must deliberately nurture and engage with, if we are to step into our true identities as creative people. Creativity is a potent force, with transformative powers, but it is a force that we must *choose* to cultivate. To me, this means that we can elect to live a creative life, one in which we are consciously attuned to the arrival of inspiration's mystery and that if we do so, we will be rewarded with unpredictable joys. By approaching creative endeavours with alacrity, we open ourselves to the possibility of attendant inspiration – we can seize and welcome ideas as they come to us. It has certainly been my own experience that when I consciously seek creative inspiration and accept serendipity, I find myself feeling inspired in often unexpected ways. An idea will come to me on my morning run; I will notice the light dance in an unusual way as I walk my youngest son home from school; a paragraph in a book I'm reading will leap out at me; or I'll hear a snippet of dialogue on the radio that sparks a different train of thought. Perhaps, as you read this, you are thinking to yourself 'Oh, but this doesn't apply to me – I'm not a creative person.' I understand. A few years ago, I would have thought exactly the same thing myself. But I'm here to tell you that you *are* a creative person. I believe that we all are. If you had asked me a decade ago if I was a creative person, I would almost certainly have laughed and said that no, I absolutely wasn't. It's taken me many years to gain my creative confidence. We are each on our own creative journey – let me tell you a little about mine.

The last time that I clearly remember drawing for pleasure was at the age of six. I sat on a village green, outside the picturesque Suffolk cottage in which my family were staying for the week, and sketched the stone-walled church. After that (somewhere along the way) I decided that I was a person who 'couldn't' draw. The image on my paper never matched up to the image in my head and from this I concluded that I was not, nor could I ever be, creative. I felt this despite the imaginative games I played with my little brother, the endless stories that I scribbled in notebooks and the sewing projects that I did with my mum.

My next memorable creative experience was at secondary school, where I surprised myself by enjoying studying textiles. I delighted in the colours and the textures, finding myself free to learn and explore using batik, tie-dye, appliqué and a range of other techniques. Meanwhile, outside school, I was also teaching myself photography. I loved my camera, but I found composing pictures and deciding what to photograph to be a challenge. I didn't know how to get it right, and for this serious, bookish girl, that was a strange sensation.

It took me years to understand the concept of shooting photographs with my heart as much as with my head and even longer to realize that the feeling of a photograph is just as important as the look of it. At university, I signed up to use the tiny photographic darkroom that was hidden away at the top of the student union building. I loved its quiet sanctuary, the heady acrid smell of the chemicals, the silence and the dark. Once, I took a friend of mine with me up the many flights of stairs. I thought that he, out of everyone, might understand the enchantment of watching the images swimming into view in the developer tray, the pleasure of the glossy black and white prints pegged on the line to dry. Years later, that boy became my husband.

SHINE, DARLING   ELLA FREARS   O·R·B
WHAT KIND OF WOMAN   POEMS   KATE BAER

ELIZABETH JENNINGS   *Selected Poems*   CARCANET

POEMS AND PROSE   CHRISTINA ROSSETTI

WALLACE STEVENS • SELECTED POEMS   FABER

WOMEN'S POETRY OF THE 1930s
A CRITICAL ANTHOLOGY   EDITED BY
                        JANE DOWSON

SYLVIA PLATH   *Collected Poems*

──THE BLOODAXE BOOK OF──
CONTEMPORARY WOMEN POETS   EDITED BY
                            JENI COUZYN   BLOODAXE

The Faber Book of
20th CENTURY WOMEN'S POETRY
Edited by Fleur Adcock

Robert Browning's Poetry

T.S.ELIOT   *Collected Poems 1909-1962*

HERA LINDSAY BIRD   HERA LINDSAY BIRD

W. H. AUDEN   *Selected Poems*

HELEN DUNMORE   INSIDE THE WAVE

William Carlos Williams   Selected Poems

THE FABER BOOK
OF MODERN VERSE

Hollie McNish   Plum

ross gay · catalog of unabashed gratitude

CREATIVITY IS AN ESSENTIAL
PART OF WHO WE ARE.

*Alongside my photography journey, my creativity found
its voice in crafts. I kept my interest in sewing and when
my eldest son was a baby my mother-in-law taught me
to knit. Knitting, more than anything, taught me to take
pleasure in the process of creation. All this time, I'd been
writing – keeping diaries and filling stacks of notebooks.
Despite my many ongoing creative pursuits, I'm not sure
I can pinpoint the moment that I understood I didn't need
permission to recognize myself as a creative person. It was
an understanding, I think, that crept up on me gradually.
I still can't use a pencil to accurately tame the image that's
in my head, but it doesn't matter. I can realize my vision
in a myriad of different ways: with yarn, or fabric, in a
cake with eggs and flour, with an arrangement of flowers
from the garden or with my words and photographs. My
creative journey is in many ways just beginning, but I
have at last recognized that my creativity is a part of
who I am. This is a blessing that touches every area of my
life. I am a creative person and – in one way or another
– I was born to create.*

We are *all* born to create. Creativity is not a gift that only a
precious few receive, it is an inherent part of human nature, a
key characteristic of our species. Each one of us is brimming with
creative potential, a potential that we alone can unlock. Creativity,
despite its mysterious nature, is not unusual. It is a fundamental part
of who we are – every person is intrinsically creative. When we were
children, creativity came as naturally to us as breathing; play was a
means of communication, a method of learning and an expression of
self. In my early twenties, I spent a few years as an infant teacher in
a tiny rural primary school, an experience which became the starting
point for my ongoing interest in play and, later, storytelling. During
my teacher training, I studied the developmental psychologist Lev
Vygotsky, who believed children's play contains the origins of the
creative imagination. Creativity begins with play and play also forms
the basis of storytelling. I observed that when the young children in
my class were absorbed in creative play, their imaginations allowed

them to step right into a story: telling, re-telling, practising and living it. Storytelling is a lifelong creative act; as we grow older, we may stop imagining stories, but we never stop telling them. I believe that regaining a sense of playfulness is a crucial way in which we can feed and encourage our latent creativity in adulthood. You have incredible (possibly untapped) creative potential, and so do I. We are born to create, but we need to learn to see ourselves as creators. Making a decision to retain an open-hearted sense of playfulness, particularly with our creative pursuits, is one way in which we can begin to reveal those treasures within.

Considering Creativity

In your journal, use the following prompts to reflect upon your personal relationship with creativity.

- What were you curious about as a child?
- What do you feel curious about right now?
- When you think of creativity, what emotions do you experience?
- What inhibits your creativity?
- What releases your creativity?
- What everyday activity do you undertake that allows you to be playful?
- What could you do today that allows you to embrace your messy side?
- What do you think would be the benefits of living a more creative life?

When you have completed the exercise, take a little time to reflect on your answers and consider if there is one practical step that you could take as a result.

Learning to pay mindful attention to the present moment – which we explored in Chapter Two – is also an important element of creativity. Ellen J. Langer says that thinking mindfully can help us to overcome any obstacles and internal prejudices that prevent us from developing into our creative selves. She writes that 'to be mindfully engaged is the most natural, creative state we can be in'.[10] Mindfulness can help us to see the world around us clearly, a key starting point for creative endeavours. In order to photograph an apple, for example, it is first necessary to *see* the apple. Learning to still the mind can lead to creative focus. With creativity, as with storytelling, we hope for balance between our inner and outer worlds – we are seeking to look closely at what we see around us, but also to listen carefully to the voice within us. However, there is a tension between stilling the thoughts to create a peaceful mind and allowing thoughts to flow freely (as we ponder, daydream and muse). Mindfulness can provide focus, but free-flowing thoughts can provide inspiration; creativity flourishes when we find a balance between the two. Strengthening our connection to the inner stream of consciousness can help us to access our creativity. Your creative process draws on *all* elements of yourself and your experiences: inspiration and motivation may come from difficulty or from sorrow. Creativity can be a distraction, but it is not always an escape – it can originate from a place of darkness, as well as from a place of light. I recognize this response from points in my own creative journey – it's not easy to tell the story of a poignant, or even a heartbreaking moment, but finding a flicker of inspiration or self-expression in sadness has helped me over the years.

Cultivating creativity is a way of life. Creative self-expression isn't restricted to making art, it can become part of the way that we live every single day. A creative lifestyle involves responding to experiences with an imaginative and open-hearted spirit. As Henri Matisse said, creativity takes courage. It takes the courage to open ourselves up to inspiration; the courage to get messy; the courage to make mistakes; the courage to play, to learn, to look within ourselves, to see both the darkness and the light and, ultimately, to be transformed. Summoning courage can feel daunting, but I would suggest that we begin (once again), by paying attention. As you pay attention to the world around you, and as you listen to the voice within you, notice what interests you. Is there a colour, object or sound that you're particularly drawn to, a topic you are keen to research, a question you long to answer or a skill you want to develop? Follow this flicker of interest, however gentle it may be, and indulge it. Look closer, listen harder. Nurture your inquisitiveness and look for connections, for a flutter of excitement, for the whisper of a story. Let your attention lead you and curiosity will be your guide.

Sparking Creative Curiosity

If you feel creatively uninspired, try one or more of the tricks below to spark your curiosity.

- Take a daydream break: allow yourself five minutes in your day to gaze out of the window and let your thoughts drift.

- Try a new creative discipline: experiment with a method of creating that contrasts with your usual creative style. Have a go at finger-painting, crochet, pottery, spoon carving... anything that you've not experimented with before.

- Go for a walk: walking, particularly in nature, is a time-honoured way to kickstart creative thoughts and ideas.

- Listen to music: instrumental music in particular provides both inspiration and an opportunity for your mind to drift.

- Start an inspiration scrapbook: sometimes, inspiration strikes at inopportune moments, such as when you are halfway through another project. If you get into the habit of collecting together magazine snippings, pictures, scraps of conversation or website links that spark your curiosity, you can return to them when you find yourself in need of inspiration.

- Go on an adventure: whether it's exploring a new path, visiting an art gallery or taking the train to a different destination, an adventure – no matter how small – is the perfect way to spark your curiosity.

We can move closer to achieving our creative potential if we open ourselves up to the possibility of inspiration, without being deterred by the lack of it. Part of creativity is certainly catching the unexpected sparkle of a sudden idea, but another part of it is persistence – choosing to engage in creative activities when we feel uninspired or even frustrated. We benefit from learning, practising and putting ourselves in the path of inspiration. In storytelling terms, I would suggest that this means developing a daily creative habit. Examples of these would be the Everyday Photography Challenge that I describe in Chapter One, or the Journalling with Emotion daily journalling exercise that I describe in Chapter Three. These practices involve committing to take a photograph, or to record a journal entry every day. In deliberately choosing to tell a little story daily, you not only develop your skills in writing and photography, you also encourage yourself to engage – both with the world around you and the voice within. If you use social media you could choose to post one little story a day for a fixed period of time (e.g. a month). Setting yourself a challenge gives your curiosity a nudge: it encourages you to look closely and to seek the extraordinary amongst the ordinary. On some days, you may feel uninspired – the story you tell may be brief – but the more that you allow for the possibility of inspiration, the more you will find yourself to be inspired, perhaps in unexpected ways. Creativity can feel like a gift, but it also has roots in discipline. In order to write this book, I sit daily at my desk, regardless of whether or not I feel inspired. I remind myself not to be afraid of the blank page and I resist the temptation to pick up my phone. I tell myself to listen; I wait for the words to come. Whatever our chosen medium, sparks of creativity originate from the ever-shifting interplay between persistence and inspiration; we need both these elements for our creative selves to flourish. If you do make a commitment to tell your little stories and nurture your own creativity, even for just a few minutes a day, I feel sure that you will be rewarded. You may even find that you are astonished.

Creativity can originate from a place of discipline, but it can also come from a place of joy – creating not for an end goal, but for a feeling of satisfaction or even unbridled delight. Creativity takes myriad forms – from art, cookery and craft, to poetry, dance and science. Writing and photography are creative practices in themselves, but we can also use them to tell the story of our creative endeavours in any form they take. Whatever your favourite creative pastime – whether it's knitting, natural dyeing, collecting beach treasures or baking bread – explore and record your creative process by telling the oh-so-little stories of what you do and how you do it. Your creative process is not just a source of intrinsic satisfaction, it is also an interesting story in itself. By all means, showcase your finished product, but also record *how* you created it; for yourself, it's a useful record and a possible learning exercise but, if you tell your stories to an audience, for them it's an insight into your creative mind. The fascinating mess of the physical creative process – the unspooling yarn, the vat of onion-skin dye, the jumbled bowl of sea glass or the flour-sprinkled tabletop – makes for compelling photographic images. Personally, when I am knitting or baking, I also find that keeping a notebook on hand not only allows me to record necessary details such as stitch counts or dough proving times, but it provides a place for me to jot down other ideas that occur to me as my mind is soothed by the gentle rhythms of physical creation.

Changing the Context to Reveal the Extraordinary in the Ordinary

Telling the little stories of our lives calls for us to *look* for magic, but sometimes I like to indulge my creativity and *make* a little. You don't have to use Photoshop to inject a touch of whimsy into your photography. Some thoughtful planning and a sprinkling of imagination are all that's needed to tell a story that transports the viewer.

I'm interested in creating photographs that blur the boundary between indoors and outdoors, images that take an ordinary moment and make it feel extraordinary. To do this, I think of a simple scene and then change its context. My favourite story to tell is a breakfast. I set a table with a simple cloth, coffee and croissants – so far, so unremarkable – but the twist is that the table is not in a kitchen or a dining, but outside in the open air. Of course, I didn't originate the idea of an outdoor table setting – this is merely my take on it. What I find interesting about this style of creative photography is that it can be immediately transporting to the viewer. A familiar scene in an unfamiliar context seems to allow us to imagine how it would be to sit down at that table and take a sip of hot coffee. It feels like a dream and, on more than one occasion, that's how it's been described to me by passing walkers who stumbled across me setting up my scene! An outdoor table setup is completely ephemeral – remaining in place for as long as it takes the coffee to cool, and then gone, leaving no trace. Each moment, each extraordinary story that I tell, is individual and transient.

Of course, I'm not suggesting that you carry a table and chairs up a hill (although if you do try it, my tip is to use a folding card table, which is easier to transport!) but for this exercise, I'd like you to plan and make a creative photograph that changes the context of an ordinary moment. You can interpret this in any way that you like, but you could consider blurring the inside/outside boundary by photographing an activity that's usually indoors (eating breakfast, sitting on a chair, going to bed, reading a book, brushing your teeth, watching a movie…) and devising a way to recreate it outdoors. Alternatively, you could consider ways in which to bring the outside in (this may rather depend on your tolerance for mess!). Another way to approach this is to use yourself (or a friend) and your outfits to tell a story and to create contrast, for example, by wearing a ballgown outdoors in a field or park, or a rain jacket and welly boots inside. You may wish to start small and simple, perhaps by photographing a stack of books on a city wall or country stile, or by planting a flower in a heap of earth on your kitchen table. It's not the scale of the image that's important – it's the flight of imagination.

The aim here is to be playful and have fun – there's no right or wrong way to create this kind of image, and the process of planning and setting it up is, in itself, an adventure. As with any creative endeavour, there are often unexpected surprises (a passing dog once wolfed down the cake I'd baked, for example!), but creative freedom is a joy and I look back on these photographs more fondly than almost any others I've taken. Of course, these are stories that I'm creating, rather than simply *recording*, but they are stories that come from my own particular imagination. Sometimes, a tiny twist is all it takes for us to see the world we take for granted in a whole new light. That – I think – makes for a story worth telling.

SOMETIMES, A TINY TWIST IS ALL IT
TAKES FOR US TO SEE THE WORLD
WE TAKE FOR GRANTED IN A
WHOLE NEW LIGHT.

Storytelling and creativity have always been intertwined. E.O. Wilson theorises that storytelling is likely to have played a crucial role in the evolution of creativity and its development as an essential part of human nature. The ancestors of our species, he suggests, would have gathered around the fire in the evenings. Fire – light, heat, sanctuary, life-source – was probably also a place for storytelling. Our human ancestors are presumed to be hunter-gatherers and many of their stories would in all likelihood have been 'mythlike accounts of actual hunts', which were listened to by all and recited over and over.[11] Storytelling became a unifying force: a source of connection and an important element in the development of human imagination. The human mind, as it has evolved, has continued to convert experience into story. Now, in the twenty-first century, imagination feels close to limitless and human creativity is sprawling and varied. In its essence, *all* creativity is about storytelling. Whatever we create, and however we create it, in doing so, we tell something of the story of ourselves, the story of how we feel, and the story of what it means to be human. Art, like storytelling, is a way of saying not just *this is how it feels to be me*, but also *this is how it feels to be alive*. Each of us has our own creative voice, and everything we create will have a style that is subtly unique to us, a style that with practice becomes stronger and more pronounced. Whatever the medium, your creative work reveals your particular creative fingerprint – it tells a story that is yours alone.

Creativity flourishes when we pay attention both to the world outside us and the voice within. Striking a balance between our inner self and the external universe is key to the act of creation. We need insight to understand what lies within us, coupled with imagination to perceive what lies beyond. Creativity asks that we become comfortable with uncertainty and be unafraid of the unknown. Creativity is mysterious and although we may not entirely understand it, the creative process itself – however unpredictable and messy it may be – is as important and beneficial as the created product. In recognizing this, we will find pleasure and fulfilment all along our creative path. Connecting with your creativity is an ongoing journey – a search that may lead you both deep inside yourself and far out, to the limits of your understanding. Creativity contains elements of storytelling and storytelling contains elements of creativity.

Once again, let's start small. Telling *your* little stories, with words and with pictures, is the perfect creative starting point. Julia Cameron, author of *The Artist's Way*, wrote that 'art is born in attention. Its midwife is detail.'[12] Over the past few chapters, we have considered why it's important to pay attention. Developing a keen sense of focus is not only a mindfulness technique, it is also part of the creative act and a step towards reaching a state of creative *flow*. Being fully in the moment can develop our storytelling but – more than this – it can allow us to create art. In the next chapter we're going to look carefully, draw in even closer and discover one of storytelling's greatest secrets: we'll find it in the details.

Seeing Things
Differently

Details matter.

They are what make stories come alive. Without the inclusion of specific details, a story has no power, no centre, no heart. Details are the way in which a storyteller ensures that a story is meaningful; they anchor it to a specific time and place, to one particular life. They prevent a story from feeling generic, boring or vague. It is the details in a story that allow us, as readers, to understand and to connect to the storyteller – one human heart with another. The tiny details that make up a life – your life – are significant. They are what make you and your story unique; the details of your individual existence are worthy of record. One of the secrets of storytelling is that the truth of a story is contained in its details. For a story to be interesting and emotionally resonant with its audience, the storyteller needs to make the details sing. Just one, single compelling detail can transfigure a story, making it feel both relevant and timeless. In his lecture, *The Aims of Art*, William Morris said that 'the true secret of happiness lies in taking a genuine interest in all the details of daily life'.[1] Daily details can be elevated through art, becoming something higher. In storytelling, daily details represent something greater and more interesting than they do when considered alone.

A well-chosen detail could be an object – perhaps one that is worn-out and loved, or unusual, new and exciting. It might have intrinsic personal meaning to you, it might be something unexpected that you have found or been given or it might be a familiar, often overlooked object that represents the rhythms of your everyday. Details can also convey sense impressions – a detail could be a smell, sound, taste or texture. Author and story guru Bobette Buster calls a single detail that encapsulates the feeling of a story, the 'gleaming detail'. She describes this occurring when an ordinary moment or object 'captures and embodies the essence of the story'[2], as if the gleaming detail represents the truth at the heart of a story. Crucial details have also been described as 'telling details' (a phrase originally attributed to Chekov, but one that I learned from writer Beth Kephart). Telling details are illuminating details that reveal a great deal in a single detail, often using just a few words. They are specific and unique to the particular story that is being told. A gleaming or telling detail reaches out to the reader and pulls them in closer, connecting them the beating heart of the story.

For me, in the story that I told about saltwater swimming in Chapter Three, the significant detail is the 'flask of scalding coffee laced with brandy' that my recently widowed grandmother held, as she waited on the beach whilst we ran headlong into the freezing December waves. The flask is practical – coffee ready to be poured in a steaming stream into cups clutched by sea-frozen, waiting hands, a hot drink being the best way to warm a body cold from the sea – but it also has emotional significance. The brandy-laced coffee is warming in both the literal and the spiritual sense. It represents something steadying to cling to in a time of grief and during an outpouring of love. It is a balm to be shared with the assembled family; a fortification and a comfort. To me, the detail of the flask speaks of something greater than itself. I hope that it serves to connect the reader with the strength, love and grief at the heart of my little story.

Including significant details when we tell little stories from our own lives helps us to preserve specific memories. Writing about a remembered experience becomes much more accurate if you can tie it to the page with concrete details. If you are unsure how to start writing the story of a moment, cast your mind back and try beginning with a single, memorable detail. The power of the story does not come from the detail itself, it comes from your perception of the detail and the meaning that it holds for you. If you can describe this detail in a few well-chosen words, it can be the starting point for the rest of your little story. Draw yourself into the remembered moment, write about the detail as precisely as you can and let the story flow. Descriptive writing is a way to explore language and to develop an expressive prose style, but it is also a way in which we can pull a moment out of time and preserve it, as a meaningful record of a sense memory – that is, a sense experience that can trigger a memory, like the way in which a specific smell can encapsulate a whole instant and pull us back into the remembered moment as we re-experience that smell. If the details in your story are vivid and meaningful to you, they are likely to resonate with your story's readers.

The inclusion of descriptive details within a story has a demonstrable impact on the reading experience. In his book *The Science of Storytelling*, writer Will Storr talks about the neuroscience behind what happens when we read stories. He writes that 'we experience the stories we read by building hallucinated models of them in our heads'. Inside our brains, as we read, we are re-creating the imagined world that is portrayed by the writer of the story.[3] If the writer has made use of specific detail, the reader can model the story world more effectively. 'Precise and specific description makes for precise and specific models', Storr explains.[4] So the more vivid our use of descriptive detail, the more accurately the reader of our story can imagine our story world, inside their own head. Descriptive detail connects the storyteller to the reader and melds together their inner worlds. However, details tend to make the strongest impact when used sparingly: don't be tempted to overwhelm your reader with endless description; a couple of telling details will make your little story sing.

Specific Descriptive Detail

You don't have to use flowery or poetic language to describe the meaningful details of your story. Just a few, precise and well-chosen words needed to make a detail stand out to the reader. Because we are telling our true stories, we don't need to imagine the details, we need to use our words carefully to describe them.

Tuning in to your senses is a good way to make your descriptions specific. Focus on whatever sense is most relevant to the detail you are describing. What, exactly, did it smell like, sound like, feel like to the touch, or taste like? If you are describing how it looked, what exact shade was its colour? What was its texture? Did it have visual quirks, damage or imperfections?

Choose one detail or object and write just a couple of sentences in your journal to describe it. Use your senses and be as precise as you can. Sometimes, comparing the object you are describing to something else can help to paint a more vivid picture for the reader. To do so, you could use a brief simile in your description (a simile is a direct comparison, involving 'as' or 'like'). For example, you might write that an apple was as green *as* a new blade of grass, or shiny *like* a polished pebble. As you describe your chosen detail, try to use words as sparingly and accurately as you can, in order to capture the *essence* of the thing that you are describing.

We record details with words and we can also record them with photographs. Photographer Elliot Erwitt described photography as being 'about finding something interesting in an ordinary place'. He wrote that 'it has little to do with the things you see and everything to do with the way you see them'.[5] In photography, as in writing, perception is everything. A mundane scene can tell a fascinating story, if you find a small detail that is interesting to you, for whatever reason. The way that the light falls on a child's morning hair, some damp confetti on a pavement, a tattered kite caught in a tree – the camera is a tool with which we can record interesting or poignant details, but the stories that we notice and tell will be as singular as the way in which we see life around us. In his influential book *Ways of Seeing*, John Berger describes the importance of seeing, which (when we are children) develops even before words. Seeing, he writes 'establishes our place in the surrounding world', and 'the way we see things is affected by what we know or what we believe'.[6] Seeing is a crucial way in which we interact with the world, but what we see and how we see it depends on who (and where) we are. When we take a photograph, our own unique viewpoint is inherent to the image that we produce. Berger writes that 'the photographer's way of seeing is reflected in his choice of subject'.[7] When you compose an image, you make choices (whether conscious or unconscious) about what to include in the frame and what to leave out. Your photographs express your distinct way of seeing the world. When we look at your image, we see what you saw; we connect with your photographer's eye and your way of seeing, whether we are aware of it or not.

Developing a way of seeing that allows us to uncover the interesting in the ordinary is key to telling the little stories of our lives, whether through words, pictures or both. Writer Natalie Goldberg considers that 'our lives are at once ordinary and mythical'.[8] Each life, with its routines and chores – getting dressed, catching a bus, going to work, walking home in the rain – is both utterly commonplace and completely remarkable. We, as humans, are each incredible, and the details of our lives are important and worthy of record. Details may at first glance seem to be ordinary, but we can learn to look at them in a different way, to develop a way of seeing that opens us up to their extraordinariness. In order to tell the story of an apparently mundane moment, Goldberg suggests that we should 'go to the heart of it and know it, so the extraordinary and the ordinary flash before our eyes simultaneously'.9 Details are small, but they are rich and real. They contain something far greater than themselves. If we begin to adjust our ways of seeing – and try to experience the ordinary more deeply and thoughtfully – we will see that life, in all its marvellous, messy glory, is right there in the details.

The geology of the county in which I live results in a landscape rich with fossils. On the hill above my town is a field that my children call 'the fossil field' because, over the years, we have found so many fossilized shells and even – once – an ammonite, whilst walking its familiar footpath. My fascination with fossils comes from my dad, whose keen treasure-hunting eye I have inherited, so when a friend introduced us to a different fossil-finding spot, beside the River Severn, we took my parents with us to explore. The Severn is an expansive, tidal river with a sweeping horizon. On this day, the tide was out and the sun glittered across the shallows. Faint from the distance came the scent of the sea.

As we walked along the foreshore, the children scrambled over loose rocks and the youngest boy exclaimed with excitement – he had found a 'devil's toenail' (a fossilized oyster). Beneath my feet was black mud and flat, layered rock bed. It seemed unremarkable, but I slowed my pace and began now to look more closely. There, amongst the loose stones, I too spotted the gnarled curve of a devil's toenail. I crouched down to pick it up. As I studied the ground, the rocky debris around my feet came into sharper focus: stones were many and varied. The sunlight caught the unmistakeable curve of a minute spiral ammonite fossil, no bigger than my little fingernail.

'Look at this!' came the cry from each of us in turn as we honed in on the hidden treasures scattered across the dried river mud. On a flat piece of driftwood, we started a collection: devil's toenails, ammonites (whole and fractured) and bivalve mollusc shells. Now, I saw the river with fresh eyes – this mud was not featureless, but teeming with unexpected surprises. I walked slowly, scanning the shore. Then out of the corner of my eye, I saw it. A tiny, perfect star, scattered like confetti from the sky. I picked it up and held it gently in the palm of my hand. A little five-pointed marvel. I had stopped, looked and paid attention and in return the unassuming mud offered up what felt to me like a charm. A blessing. A fallen star.

I know now (thanks to my geology book) that these stars (of which, in the end, we found several) are called crinoids: small cross-sections of the fossilized stems of hundreds of millions-of-years-old sea lilies (ancient relatives of the starfish and sea urchin). Not fallen stars, but perhaps no less remarkable. My eagle-eyed dad took his own fossil findings home to add to what the family calls his 'museum', and the children and I filled our pockets with our finds, none more precious to me than the little stellar sea lilies. Look closely – fossil-hunting has taught me – take your time, focus your gaze and you may discover a true treasure: maybe even one that has lain undiscovered for millions of years.

In order to become more consciously aware of your own way of seeing, consider what it is that draws *your* gaze. How closely do you look at the world around you? If we want to spot treasures that are concealed in plain sight, we must train our eyes to focus in and notice the details. Writer Anne Lamott reminds us of the sensation of walking alongside a young and enthusiastic child who sees the world with unabashed wonder. This is an experience that is deeply familiar to me. I have clear memories of walking with each of my three boys as young toddlers – they trotted along beside me,

DETAILS ARE SMALL, BUT
THEY ARE RICH AND REAL.

repeatedly stopping to examine and exclaim over a red leaf! A little snail! A funny pebble! The sky in a puddle! Re-living a child's way of seeing, so different from an adult's jaded viewpoint, can cause us to reassess and alter the way that we look at the world. Lamott suggests that we too should adopt a similar openness to wonder: looking to be 'present and in awe' as we move through our days. There is, she writes, 'ecstasy in paying attention'.[10] At the core of this practice of paying attention is a sensation of seeing anew – viewing the world through clear eyes, as if for the first time. What would happen if, even if just for an hour, you adopted an attitude close to childlike wonder, choosing to be freshly surprised – perhaps even delighted – by the world?

What will catch your eye and make your heart sing? Your way of seeing is an individual product of what you know, what you believe and who you are. It is completely unique to you and, as a result, so too is your storytelling voice. Ask yourself: what are the things that only you see, the little stories that you alone want to tell? This could be a good opportunity to take a walk – you may wish to return to the Mindful Photowalk exercise in Chapter Two. Seeing the wonder in something that others walk mindlessly past can make you feel as if you have discovered a remarkable secret. Often, I find the little stories that interest me when I look beyond the obvious. For example, I'm less interested in the grand façade of a building and more interested in the tiny cracked window on the side of an outbuilding. I prefer the vine weed that snakes its way around the supermarket car park to the plump, glossy roses in a perfectly manicured front garden. I look for found objects such as playing cards (they're more common than you might think!), gloves or dropped shopping lists. I notice the discarded, the overlooked and the overgrown; I'm always searching for unexpected poetry. As Roald Dahl once wrote: 'watch with glittering eyes the whole world around you because the greatest secrets are always hidden in the most unlikely places'.[11]

Embracing Serendipity

Part of opening ourselves up to wonder involves making the choice to enjoy the unexpected and to embrace the serendipitous. Serendipity (finding interesting or valuable things by chance) is not about happening upon a stray banknote (nice though this would be!). In the context of telling little stories it means chancing upon things that are interesting or valuable to you and you alone. Small discoveries that spur a particular connection or association, that lead to a feeling or emotion, that remind you of a person, place, or experience. Serendipity is impossible to plan for, but when it occurs it can feel like a gift from the universe. If we hurry around, eyes down – or glued to our phones – it can be easy to miss these unexpected gifts. Making the choice to be more present opens us up to serendipitous discoveries, whatever they may be. For me, it might be a heart-shaped stone; scattered yellow ginkgo leaves on the pavement; a fading hydrangea bush; an old wooden stool with a label reading 'free to a good home'; a feather; a few lines from a poem stencilled on a wall. For you, it will no doubt be something else. Whatever serendipity means to you, when it occurs, embrace it and consider telling its story with a photograph or a couple of sentences.

Telling little stories (despite what we may see on social media) is not about showcasing perfect lives. Quite the opposite. Perfection rarely has an interesting story to tell! Life is messy and imperfect and, as storytellers, we should try to embrace this. Mess (whether physical or emotional) is not something to be ashamed of, it is the stuff of life – an accumulation of all that makes us who we are and a part of what it means to be human. If we choose to see it as such, mess can be beautiful. As storytellers, we try to recognize this complicated, flawed, truthful beauty. Our stories reflect our lives – both in terms of the subject matter and also in terms of the creative process. Telling little stories is something that is done *by* you, *for* you. Life isn't perfect, so don't expect your journal to be. Give yourself the freedom to write without judgement and to create without constraint. If your notebook is anything like mine, there will be pages of scrawl and crossings out, ink blots and perhaps even tearstains. Equally, your camera roll is yours alone and it's an excellent place for experimentation. If you want to fill it with pictures of your feet, bicycles, the view through your window, flowers or street signs, that's entirely your choice. It will always be up to you what you share and what you keep to yourself – you don't owe anyone your stories, or your vulnerability. But if only within the pages of your journal, try to embrace the beautiful, tangled mess – it's a part of who you are, the source of your unique voice and the place where all your little stories begin.

I have found that, over time, the creative act of telling stories with words and photographs has altered the way I see the world. Partly as a result of paying mindful attention, I frequently view the world around me with a mind to taking a picture (as if seeing with a photographer's eye) or with a mind to writing about what I observe (as if seeing with a writer's eye). My own creative practices have helped me to crystallize the way in which I perceive the world and I believe that they have also actively changed the way in which I see. I find that I now attend more closely to the details – of daily life, of nature, of the seasons and of the world around me. I feel more conscious of my immediate environment, attuned to the merest hint of a story. I was interested to know how other creatives experience this, so I asked some other writers and photographers about their own ways of seeing, to find out which elements of everyday life inspired their writing or photography, and what the concept of having a writer or a photographer's eye meant to them.

Photographer Polly Alderton explained that daily details are central to her photography: 'It's not that I'm necessarily drawn to the details I photograph', she wrote, 'but more that they are my only options. I've noted before that I'm always trying to pre-empt the feeling of nostalgia and desire to recall a memory. One of my favourite things about looking at old pictures is noticing small things in the background – things that you might ordinarily hide away; piles of washing, cups waiting to be washed, certain trinkets that transitioned their way from the home over time. I'm trying always to notice the mundane – the mundane makes up for so many layers of our memory recall. I like photography because it's instant, in printing a picture the image becomes a physical thing you can hold in your hands, it has a tangibility – the translation of memory into a real thing.'

Taking time to notice the mundane is a crucial element of everyday storytelling. As Polly says, the daily details of home (the objects we easily overlook and take for granted) will one day become receptacles of memory that prompt our feelings of nostalgia. I have long admired the truthful realism of Polly's photography and her startling ability to turn family life into art. Her beautiful phrase, *the translation of memory into a real thing* offers the best argument I can think of for taking the time to print your pictures. For me, the tangibility of a photographic print is a real and attainable kind of magic.

Photographer Jo Yee wrote: 'My favourite part of the day is in the morning when it's still dark out but the haze of light is slowly emerging. The kettle is on and in a few moments the promise of coffee will be realized. I suppose I'm drawn to the stillness of the early morning, it's dark but comforting and hopeful. My photography is in the same vein.' She explained that for her, 'having a strong photographer's eye stretches past seeing good composition. It sees potential in the normal or mundane that strikes a chord with viewers.' Interestingly, Jo also uses the word 'mundane' to describe a source of photographic potential: an everyday occurrence that will cause the viewer to feel or understand something, to forge a connection with the photograph. We can all visualize the scene that Jo describes: the stillness of early morning, with steam rising from the kettle and daylight gradually appearing. These comforting and hopeful elements of everyday life are reflected in Jo's photography.

Haiti-based photographer Dominique St-Germain wrote that she 'is always looking for beauty in everything'. She often shoots her narrative self-portrait images outside. The landscape is a part of the story that she tells and she says that 'every corner of nature, every flawed curve of my environment is something that really draws my heart towards what it means to be in touch with what the universe is offering us'. She considers her photographer's eye to be 'truly a blessing' because it causes her to 'discover entire micro aesthetic universes inside our environment'. I identify with this, because I too find nature to be a source of infinite fascinating detail. In photographic terms, any landscape always offers the possibility to zoom in closer and then closer again: the chance to lose ourselves in colour, pattern, or the intricacies of plant or insect life.

Do we learn to see the world in a certain way through the practice of photography, or are we called to practice photography because of the way we see? I had wondered if photographers became drawn to photography as a medium because it reflects their natural inclination for a certain way of seeing. It could be, however, that the impulse they share is the desire to tell stories. Polly Alderton wrote that 'taking pictures is a way of solidifying my experience, a proof of what is or was if you like'. Taking pictures is a form of creative

expression. It is a way to contain and record experience, to capture moments and make memories into physical reality. Drawing or writing are different ways in which to achieve a similar end.

Novelist Rachel Edwards described the everyday details that stimulate her creativity: 'Those sudden flashes of joy or irritation – anything that elicits a strong emotion; a news story that makes me sit up, or groan; a memorable meal, or a taste that triggers Proustian recall; a chance comment by a loved one; a single bar of music or an image that rocks me.' Being a writer, she explained, 'means always searching for meaning. Writing is a privilege: it allows you to process your observations of life and people and the world; to attempt to create a narrative from that which is important to you and which, you fervently believe, may connect with others.' For writers, whether novelists, memoirists or us with our own little stories, connection is the goal. Seeking meaning in life, then distilling and expressing this meaning so that it can be communicated to others, is the writer's quest. Author Shirley Jackson once wrote that writers see everything 'through a thin mist of words'[12] – we notice things and, in our minds, we attempt to describe them, whether or not we have a pen in hand. All stories, large or small, take something which is important to the storyteller as a starting point, and then attempt to communicate it in a way that connects with the story's readers. Feeling the flash of creative inspiration in an everyday moment can offer us the beginning of a little story.

Memoirist Eliska Tanzer describes the writer's search for meaning: 'I look for the subtlety or the hidden meanings behind certain things.' Writers hone their ability to look below the surface of moments or events, searching out deeper meanings and hidden stories. Novelist Emma Christie says: 'I like listening to the way people speak and present themselves to others – whether it's taxi drivers, clients, family, colleagues – and what they're really trying to tell you. I used to work as a news reporter so was trained to really listen, and often the real story is hidden underneath the one that people are telling you.' Writing, whether fiction or memoir, is about listening and looking for this *real story*, the story with emotional resonance, the story that has the ability to connect to a reader. As we reflect on the stories of our own lives, perhaps we too can learn to dig a little deeper and consider not just the events that immediately come to mind, but also the ideas that might be hidden below the surface – the meaning in the depths. Emma writes that 'everyone is a storyteller and, as a writer I can learn a lot by simply paying attention to the lives of ordinary people'. Once again we are reminded of the importance of paying attention – observation is crucial to a search for meaning, the central purpose of the writer's craft. We (keepers of journals, lovers of notebooks) are storytellers too and there is much we can learn from simply paying attention to our own ordinary lives.

As I write now, I notice raindrops sliding down my windowpane in the early dusk. They glitter in the last of the day's light, weaving across and around each other in a gentle, sliding dance. It is the end of an utterly ordinary Tuesday afternoon in winter. The sky beyond my window is glowering, grey and completely unremarkable, but this dance of the raindrops, although commonplace, is strangely mesmerizing to me. The raindrops sliding down the glass speak to me of life's unexpected poetry, a manifestation of that ecstasy of paying attention. Raindrops are a tiny, easily overlooked detail which, to my way of seeing, have a story to tell – a flash of magic in the mundane. I have seen raindrops on my window a hundred times before and I will see them (I hope) a hundred times again, but on this particular day, I am drawn to them, finding them worthy of record. I believe that when you tell your little stories, being true to the details is a way of being true to yourself. Your unique way of seeing is reflected in the specific aspects that you are drawn to, just as it is reflected in your unique storytelling voice. The flash of the extraordinary within the ordinary is often fleeting. Moments pass, the sky has faded to navy blue and the raindrops have disappeared from view, but here on the page, they remain.

A Diary of Light

One way in which to see with a photographer's eye is to start to actively notice the light. For photographers, an awareness of light is almost like a sixth sense – and it can become a beautiful obsession. The sparkle of the golden hour, the soft glow of sunset, the dancing rays that make their way across your kitchen wall: perfect light – when you find it – is thrilling, beguiling and as addictive as a drug. My children (ever-patient photographer's subjects) often hear me call out: 'Can you come here a moment for a picture? I've found a patch of pretty light.'

The best light for photographs is almost always natural daylight, rather than artificial light. As photographers, we cannot control the light, but we can learn to employ it to best advantage in our images, always considering how we can use the light available to us in order to tell a story which highlights the subject of our image. Learning to use the light begins with *seeing* it – noticing it in all its guises, observing it and succumbing to its seductive charms.

Whether your camera is in your hand or not, as you go about your day, try to train yourself to think in terms of light. Ask yourself: Where is the light coming from right now? Is it bright or muted, full or dappled, cloud-soft or sun-flared? What is it doing? How is it changing? When you learn to really notice the light, you will begin to realize that often, when it comes to taking a photograph, the light is the story.

For this task, I'd like you to keep a photographic diary of light – a light collection, if you will. Over the next week, try to observe and photograph as many different types of light as you can. Try to capture an image of bright sunlight , the soft light of cloud cover, the sparkling light of the golden hour (the hour before sunset or after sunrise). Observe how the light travels across the walls of your house, and photograph its patterns. Look for soft dappled sunlight in the shade of a tree and the full force of the midday sun. Notice how light bounces off walls, drops down from doorways and diffuses through glass. Collect as many different examples of light as you can.

At the end of the week, look through your images and consider how they make you feel. What stories does the light tell? Have you discovered light spots or types of light that you particularly love? How could you make use of these as you tell your little stories? You may find that – like me – your search for the light will become an ongoing one and your light collection will continue to grow. I know that love for the light will forever be a part of who I am and how I see.

Finding Your
Creative Voice

What makes your story remarkable is the way that you tell it.

Your voice is as unique and indelible as your fingerprints and it's an unmistakeable part of who you are. Just as your speaking voice is distinct and instantly recognizable to those who know you, the same can be true of your creative voice – whether written or visual. Over time, you acquire a tone that is particular to you, one that conveys your character and personal qualities, as well as your individual style. Developing this authentic and consistent voice takes practice, and learning to listen. In her 2013 Commencement address at Harvard University, Oprah Winfrey emphasized the importance of listening to the 'still small voice' within yourself, in order to 'find out what makes you come alive'.[1] This, she suggested to her audience, is the key to being happy, successful and making a difference in the world. Over the past few chapters we have considered ways in which we can begin to tune in to this still, small inner voice. The time has come, then, to ask that voice – to ask ourselves – a question: *what makes me come alive?*

The stories that you choose to tell, and the moments that you choose to record, are a reflection of what it is that you personally find interesting and compelling. As storytellers – as humans – we are products of our obsessions, whatever they may be. Consider the things in life (from minute to massive) that fascinate you, that draw you in and light you up. What touches your curiosity and ignites your interest? What do you look out for, dream about, ponder over or delight in? What makes you come alive? Obsessions can be general (a favourite colour, a country, a particular weather condition), or they can be incredibly specific (a collection of records by one artist, a dish you love to cook, an item of clothing that you wear over and over). Obsessions hold innate potential. This comes not from that which obsesses us, but from the strength of our preoccupation and the way in which our passion and fascination will inevitably be woven into who we are. Exploring, expanding upon and seeking to understand your own personal obsessions may reveal new connections, as you develop a clearer understanding of who you are and what inspires you.

A Collection

Let's consider collections. A collection is a group of objects of one type. It doesn't matter whether those objects are priceless paintings, silver teaspoons, books, stamps, shells, ornaments, badges or pebbles – what makes them interesting is the stories that they tell about the person who has collected them.

I'd like you to consider a collection of yours – one that you have now, or that you had as a child – and answer the following questions in your journal.

- What is/was the collection of?
- Where is/was it stored or displayed?
- How large is/was it?
- How long did it take you to acquire this collection?
- Did you consciously begin collecting, or did you find that your collection developed organically?
- What does/did your collection represent to you?
- If this was a childhood collection, is there an element of it that you'd like to return to and bring into your present life in some way and, if so, how?
- If it is a current collection, how do you see yourself growing or expanding it in the future?

Tell the story of one or two specific pieces from your collection: describe them, explain how and why you acquired them, reflect on how you felt when they became part of your collection.

How do you think that this interest of yours makes you come alive? How is its influence reflected in your creative voice?

Personally, I am an inveterate collector (a hoarder, some might say). My collections track the course of my preoccupations and interests. From my crafting days, I have a huge jar of rainbow-coloured plastic knitting needles, purchased a pair at a time from local charity shops. Lined up on the top of my kitchen dresser is a small collection of blue and white French jugs, hunted out from flea-market sales during many summers of family holidays in France. I accumulate unframed oil paintings and vintage cameras, and my collection of found natural objects grows almost daily: sea glass, quartz pebbles, hagstones, driftwood, shells and seedheads are all irresistible to me. My obsessions also are scattered through my camera roll – I can never pass a pretty old window, a reflected patch of light or a misty landscape, without taking a picture. I look down and snap photographs of my feet as I move through the world: in a pile of autumn leaves, on the edge of a sea pool, or on a lovely tiled floor. Each obsession encapsulates many layers of stories. If you are unsure as to what your own obsessions are, look around your home, scroll through your camera roll, flick through your notebooks. What is precious to you? What concerns you? Look for your genuine interests, for the themes or subjects that recur time and again. You may not be able to articulate *why* you find these things interesting, but for now, just observe that you do. Your obsessions are the place where your stories begin. Start the next little story you tell with one of your obsessions or preoccupations. 'You were made and set here', Annie Dillard wrote, 'to give voice to this, your own astonishment'.[2] The practice of telling little stories – of telling your stories – is a way in which you can give voice to your astonishment. Paying attention (to our obsessions, to the world outside and to the voice within) leads, Mary Oliver told us it would, to being astonished. Your creative voice expresses this singular astonishment – it tells the particular story of what makes *you* come alive.

In my early twenties, I spent a year studying for a Master's degree in Poetry. I lived in a little one-bedroom flat in an old house beside a church. My desk was in a corridor, wedged into a funny cubbyhole, where my ancient computer jostled for space with piles of hand-scrawled notes. The bay windows in the sunny sitting room were flanked by wobbling stacks of poetry books, well-thumbed and annotated in pencil. To help fund my studies, I spent a couple of days each week working in a bookshop, delighting in the hush of a roomful of books. During that time, I lived and breathed poetry, reading it, pondering it, discussing it with my course-mates in the book-lined studies of our tutors, with whispered conferences in libraries and chats in corners of cosy pubs. We offered each other poems like little gifts, reading, re-reading and sharing our favourites.

After I graduated, my poetry books were packed away into boxes. Life moved on. I got a job, bought a house, got married, had children. It happens, though, that a love of poetry never leaves you. It took me a good while before I began to read it for pleasure again, but now the bookshelf beside my bed is home to a treasured collection of slim volumes of poetry and I have discovered poetic voices beyond the narrow canon that my university taught. It's not confined to my bookshelf, however; I believe that poetry is also a part of my creative voice.

When I say this, I don't mean that I am a poet – far from it. In fact, my understanding of poetry has convinced me that the ability to write good poems is not something that I possess! But as time has passed, I have begun to observe that my fondness for poetry has quietly and unexpectedly infused my creative voice. In both my writing and my photographs, I credit poetry for my love of gentle melancholy and my appreciation of poignant transience. I attribute to it my interest in the precision of language and my constant quest to find the clearest and most expressive phrases. Poetry has given me the courage to

YOUR OBSESSIONS ARE THE PLACE
WHERE YOUR STORIES BEGIN.

experiment with words, to tumble them together, to know when they feel right – even if they are not strictly correct. Poetry taught me that the smallest things are worthy of record. From poets, I have learned to lean in to my obsessions, to look for meaning in the moment and to examine myself and my motivations. I have discovered that words are a means through which I can explore and begin to understand and express the truth of my own feelings and experiences.

Poetry, to me, is not just words on a page. It is a quality of beauty or intensity that can also be expressed with images. It is found in unexpected places and amongst everyday things. The little stories that I tell, and the creative voice with which I tell them, owe so much to those days spent in book-lined rooms, or hunched up at my corridor-desk. I thought I had been learning about poetry, but all along I was learning how to be myself.

Your voice is infused not just with what you love and treasure, but with where you have been, what you have seen, what you have learned, experienced and done. It expresses who you are. The more notebooks that you fill, the more photographs that you take, the more stories that you tell, the stronger your voice will become. Over time you may find that, with practice, you are able to hold your work at arm's length and listen, to read your words and hear your own voice echoing back at you. Listening for your voice does not require you to judge your creative output, it asks you to reflect on the influences and inflections that make your voice your own. If everyone who attended an event were to share their version of this story, what would make your telling of its story unique and unmistakably you? Consider what it is that distinguishes your written voice: the words, tone, style, subject matter, emotional intensity and personality that are blended together to make it your own. In a similar way, many of these elements will determine what makes your visual voice distinctive.

THERE IS POWER IN THE OPENING
SENTENCE OF A STORY, HOWEVER
SMALL THAT STORY MIGHT BE.

Developing a Visual Storytelling Voice

In order to explore your own visual voice, it is beneficial to consider some of your photographs together – as an overarching story, or developing body of work. Gather together 10 favourite photographs that you have taken. You could do this on your computer, you could print them out and spread them across your table, or (if Instagram is somewhere you showcase your images) you could study your Instagram feed.

Look carefully at your photographs as you see them together and, in your journal, jot down answers to the following questions:

- What are the dominant colours?
- Do the tones of the photographs appear warm or cold?
- Are the colours muted or bright?
- What type of images are these? (e.g. portrait, landscape, close-up, interiors, action, still-life, etc.)
- What recurring themes or subjects do you notice?
- Write down three words that unite and describe this particular set of photographs (e.g. moody, dreamy, stark, whimsical, urban, heart-warming, quiet, documentary, etc.)

There will probably be some elements of your visual voice as represented by these images that you would like to embrace and develop and some that you would like to change. Your visual voice may not currently be strong and distinctive – it may be a faint whisper that is beginning to emerge. This is fine. Our creative skills do not always match up to our creative vision. Uniting what we *imagine* and what we *can do* takes time.

You are on a creative storytelling journey. Practice, although it may not make perfect, brings you closer to producing images that capture what you visualize; the more visual stories you tell, the stronger your visual storytelling voice will become. Having a sense of what you want your subject matter, colour palette, themes and image style to be, is an important step towards developing your own distinctive visual voice.

In your journal, write down three words that describe the visual storytelling voice you would most like to achieve (these words may be different from the words that you wrote down earlier). Try to choose words which distil a sense of how *you* see the world. Over the next few days, when you pick up your camera or phone, remind yourself of these three words and try to incorporate a feeling of one or more of them into the image that you take.

Your creative voice is the embodiment of your small, still, inner voice, the voice that makes you yourself. It is an accumulation of many elements, one of which will be your emotions. Our creative voices can originate from joy, happiness, curiosity and celebration, but they can also have their origins in anger, grief, fear or pain. The emotional source of creativity is nuanced; it comes from a complex place in which several, or all, of these elements are combined. The moments, experiences, people, places and memories that – for whatever reason – stay with us, or even haunt us, are what spur us to tell our stories. Your own creative voice comes from deep within you, from the heart of who you are.

We each employ our creative voices for a myriad of reasons: to find expression, escape, understanding, remembrance, or perhaps even redemption. Wherever your creative voice comes from, it has led you to the present moment, to the stories that you are preparing to tell. The *source* of your creative voice may not be within your power, but you can certainly influence its destination. What is it that you are writing or creating *towards*?

Anne Lamott writes of the importance of placing truth at the centre of our writing. She says that 'if something inside you is real, we will probably find it interesting, and it will probably be universal'. She instructs us to write 'straight into the emotional centre of things'.[3] Making the decision to write towards something larger than yourself – something such as truth – gives your storytelling power and purpose. Choosing a conscious direction for your words lends an intensity to your work and carries your readers along with you on your journey. As you listen more intently to the quiet, still voice inside yourself, share what you find to be powerful and real, drawing on the obsessions that compel you. Write towards the emotional centre of the little story that you wish to tell. Whether you are writing your stories for an audience, or for yourself alone, keeping the truth (as you understand it) at the heart of your writing will help you to develop your own creative voice. Telling your stories can be intimidating, I know. Try to forget, for a moment, about your words ever being read. Your journal is your own space, where you will not be judged. There are no expectations or societal pressures; it is just you, your pen, notebook, camera and the little story you are telling. Think only about what it is that you are writing towards – the truth that is at the heart of your story.

Making a quiet voice heard in a loud world can feel challenging. Sometimes, it may seem that your inner voice is drowned out by a cacophony of external voices, clamouring for attention. Elizabeth Gilbert suggests cultivating a sense of what she calls 'creative entitlement'. This means believing that 'you are allowed to have a voice and a vision of your own'.[4] We need to hold on to the belief that we have a right to express ourselves – and find the courage to assert our presence. 'My voice matters.' Whisper those words to yourself. Say them out loud. Believe them. No one but you can tell your stories in your voice. Sometimes, when my creative courage is waning, on the days (of which there are many) when I feel convinced that I have nothing to say and my story is of interest to no one, I remind myself that everything is finite. I will not be here forever – none of us will – and this moment, this chance to tell my story, may be the only one that I get. You don't need anyone's permission to tell your stories: they belong to you and you are the only one who can tell them in your voice. Your stories, my stories, all of our stories are important. In the end, our stories will outlast us – they will be what remains with those who love us, after we are gone. Nurture your sense of creative entitlement and believe in the power, the beauty and the substance of your own voice.

When you begin to write a little story, the opening sentence will immediately establish your voice. What tone comes naturally to you when you tell a story? It may be flippant and funny, heartfelt and poignant, hesitant and uncertain or flowery and descriptive. Imagine that you are telling this story out loud to a friend – how would you begin? Like your spoken voice, your storytelling voice should remain true to who you are, but it also needs to be clear, so as to communicate your message. There is power in the opening sentence of a story, however small that story might be – it is a moment of connection between storyteller and listener. This is your chance to invite your audience to draw closer, to step for a moment into your world and to listen to what you have to say. Personally, when writing a little story, I always find the first sentence to be the most difficult. I ponder my story – the bones of it, what it means to me – and I try to find the best words to pull the reader straight into it. I know that this opening sentence speaks in my voice when it *feels* right and when, once I've written it, the rest of the story begins to flow with ease. The beginning of a story is sometimes referred to as the 'hook' because it hooks the reader in, so that they continue to read. Your opening sentence is your hook – it is there to seize the reader's attention and to allow them to hear your voice.

Writing towards the truth means being true to your story, but it also means being true to your voice. Have you ever felt closely connected to a particular storyteller? Whether it's a writer, a photographer, a documentary-maker or someone that you follow on social media, if a storyteller has a compelling voice they invite you into their story, making you feel almost as if you *know* them. When we read every book by an author, seek out exhibitions by a photographer or find ourselves regularly checking in on an online storyteller, what we are drawn to is their creative voice. Think of one of your own favourite storytellers, in whatever genre. What makes their voice clear and recognizable to you? What do you love about the distinctive way in which they tell their stories? Reflecting on what distinguishes a creative voice that we love can help us to begin to establish our own. I'm not suggesting that you copy someone else's voice, rather that you consider how it is composed. Analyse their choice of subject matter, tone and details, as well as colours (for a visual voice) and word choices (for a written voice). What makes this person's voice so appealing to you? What is it about their voice that is unique? If you read a story, or look at a photograph, and immediately know that it could only have been created by *one* person, that storyteller has an unmistakeable creative voice. Now, ask yourself the same questions as they apply to your own storytelling: your aim is not to echo someone else's creative voice, but to understand what makes it recognizable and to use this knowledge to clarify and strengthen your own voice. You may find that you sense you have been drawn to this storyteller because they reflect back to you something of yourself, but your own voice belongs to you.

If you share your stories with others – if you have social media accounts, a blog, anywhere you tell stories online – your voice is the connecting thread that runs through all that you post. Communicating in your true creative voice will mean that your personality shines through. You can celebrate your sense of humour and allow your imperfections to show – it's necessary to be a little vulnerable in order to have an honest and authentic voice. Allow your audience to get to know the person behind the words or images; nothing pulls us in to your story better than occasional vulnerability. Nevertheless, there's a balance to be found between sharing from the heart and revealing too much and that balance will be different for everyone. Personally, I often elect to share photographs of beauty and serenity because, for me, my public Instagram feed is one part of my life that is untouched by mess and chaos, and keeping it largely peaceful brings me calm and creative fulfilment. I don't pretend to live a perfect life, however – I share behind-the-scenes snippets, and my vulnerability tends to surface in the captions to my images, which is where my stories are told. I also have a private Instagram account where I share more intimate moments with a handful of family and friends. This is what works for me, although it may not work for everyone. Essentially, I believe that as it's my story, I'm in charge. So are you. You don't owe anyone your whole story and you don't have to show every detail of your life, but in the little stories that you do choose to share, be true to yourself.

*O*ne spring day, a few years ago, I picked a basket of white blossom from the small tree in my front garden. The blooms on this particular tree last only a few days, so I wanted to record them with a photograph before they faded away for another year. My house, as usual, was messy and – stuck for space – I placed the basket on my distressed wooden stairs and took a shot. When I later shared the photograph on Instagram, I was astonished by how many people commented on the loveliness of my stairs. These are stairs that are scuffed and marked, splattered with paint, a fading, peeling white stripe down each side of where a carpet runner used to be. I am, I must confess, fond of them, but it had never crossed my mind that they would appeal to anyone else. And yet, there clearly was something about their imperfections – perhaps the stories that they could tell of a century's worth of feet, running up and down – that caught people's imaginations.

I experimented with using my stairs as the backdrop for another photograph, this time the elderflowers that my children and I had gathered from the local lanes so as to make cordial. Once again, the photograph was unexpectedly popular. I began to see the stairs in a whole new light. As time went on, I developed this motif further, setting myself the challenge to record the story of the passing seasons with still-life scenes arranged on my stairs. In the autumn, bright yellow beech leaves from a tree in the woods; in the winter a garland of snowy *Clematis vitalba*; in the spring, cherry blossom from the tree outside my bedroom window; in the summer, a bunch of blooms from the garden of a kind friend. My project had simple constraints: each still-life included natural objects, placed on the stairs. I was surprised by how many different stories I could tell in this way.

Developing Projects and Motifs

One way in which to experiment with your visual storytelling voice is to set yourself the challenge of an ongoing creative photography project. Sometimes, projects of this nature evolve completely organically – this is what happened with my stairs series.

Setting yourself a photography project is an excellent way in which to develop your creativity and strengthen your creative voice. I would suggest that you look back over photographs that you have previously taken and consider whether there is a particular theme, location or image type that you could replicate, develop and explore. Although I offer here a few ideas, for a project to best develop your voice it needs to be on a theme that feels natural to you, so aim for a storytelling challenge that incorporates your unique viewpoint and interests.

- Table or desk top: consider a project in which you take ongoing images of your kitchen table, or desk, and tell the story of the way it changes throughout the year.

- A corner of your home: you may not have a scruffy staircase, but perhaps you have a windowsill, chair or mantelpiece that you could use as the basis for your photography project. Can you tell the story of the seasons, using this corner as your setting?

- Books: can you find an interesting way in which to tell the story of the books you read and where you read them?

- Food: consider a project that tells the story of meals that you cook and eat (either the process of cooking or the final dish).

Choose a motif that's unique to you and tells a specific story. Set yourself some simple constraints: establish what elements of your photographs will be the same each time and what aspects you will change. Most importantly, experiment and have fun. If you share your work on social media, it may feel as if you always have to produce content that's fresh, new and different. In fact, returning to repeated motifs can actually help you to grow your audience, because they will know what to expect from you, and the familiarity of your vignettes appearing in their feed will be predictable, and even soothing.

Social media is filled with other people's aspirational highlights and it often pulls us in to an apparently perfect world, leaving us dully scrolling through what others are sharing and doing, wishing our time away. We assume that the perfection on display is the whole story, but there's always another story outside the carefully selected frame; there will more than likely be imperfection, or even chaos, just out of shot. Framing a photograph is making a choice – there are elements that are included and elements that are left out. No one's life is perfect, however much it may appear so. Outside the frame, life is messy and complicated; we are all vulnerable, so do be kind. Next time you find you are comparing yourself to someone else online, stop and notice the feeling. See if you can isolate precisely what it is that is making you feel inferior or frustrated. Is it a gorgeous home, exotic travels, a tempting-looking breakfast or an impeccably styled outfit? Or are you comparing your own photography skills or career achievements to those of someone else? Consider whether you can channel this negative feeling into positive action. Recognizing someone else's achievements can be a way in which to spur yourself forward and work towards your own. The tight feeling that I got in the bottom of my stomach when I saw fellow creatives announce book deals was one of the ways that I knew writing a book was what I *really* wanted to do. If you too get that feeling, it may help you to stop scrolling and take one small step towards your own creative or personal goal, whatever it may be. Another positive action you could consider is to reach out to the person whose post has affected you and leave a warm, appreciative comment. Real people are far less intimidating than the idealized versions that we often create in our heads, and having the courage to make contact is an opportunity to connect and perhaps to learn. However, if you find that you're experiencing comparison envy or dissatisfaction, it's probably time to take a break. You can mute or unfollow accounts that don't make you happy – your feeds should be a positive place for you. The best solution to uncomfortable feelings of comparison is simply to put down your phone and step away from social media for a while, ideally to do something tangibly creative.

When using social media, we all constantly make decisions about what to share and our individual choices may vary from day to day. On some days you may feel like sharing the sad, negative or messy elements of your experience – to inject a sense of reality, or to connect with others who feel the same way – whilst on other days you may wish only to celebrate and showcase the beauty in your life. These two approaches are not mutually exclusive. Stories, like life, can be both messy and beautiful. What weaves your stories together, and invites your audience closer, is that they are all told in your exclusive voice. You will probably find that your natural voice will draw to you those with similar interests and experiences, offering opportunities for connection. However, social media is an opportunity to connect not just with those whose lives mirror yours, but also with people whose voices, backgrounds and experiences differ from your own. This does not tend to happen by accident. We make a choice to seek out, discover and engage with people who have varied voices. When we listen to, interact with and share stories told by people with different backgrounds from our own, we are enriched. We can learn, empathize, build friendships and begin to see things differently. Social media storytelling offers us connection, compassion and – through hearing and engaging with the voices of others – the opportunity to recognize, learn, understand, collaborate, share new perspectives and discover different stories.

As you write a story, you will be aware of its intended audience, whether it's your online followers, your family or your future self. Your public voice may be subtly different from your free, unfettered, private voice – the voice that you record in your notebooks. A journal offers a space in which to write without judgement: in your journal, you tell stories to yourself. Over time, a journal can become both an exploration of your voice and also a rich source of potential material for your creative storytelling, or for other projects. The creative voice originates from (and communes with) that quiet inner voice, which is more readily expressed in the privacy of a personal journal. An ongoing storytelling practice is a way in which to record not just who you are, but also over time, to understand who you once were. This is true of personal storytelling with words and also with photographs. Even the most established and distinctive creative voices will be fluid over time; developing a creative voice is a lifelong journey.

Your experiences and perspective are constantly evolving and so too is your unique voice. What makes your story remarkable is the way that you tell it and yet – as writer Rebecca Solnit reminds us – 'we think we tell stories, but stories often tell us'.[5] The world around us is an invisible web of stories, a sprawling, gossamer network of tales that connect, guide and can even control us. Your little stories are a tiny part of this expansive universe of stories. In order to harness our own little stories so that we can tell them effectively, we must understand something of the power of story.

The Power
of Story

The universe as we know it is held together by stories.

They are a constant presence in every aspect of our lives. They help us to navigate – and to find the meaning in – daily existence. We don't just experience stories through fiction (in books, films, television dramas and plays); the news is presented to us in the form of stories, as is history and also national identity. Stories are our constant preoccupation; they are the way in which we comprehend our entire world. Each of us exists within the nebulous construct of our own life story, which is itself composed of many, many little stories. We dwell on them, or sometimes we try to forget them. We exchange them with friends, in pubs, cafés or at the school gates. We share them around the supper table at the end of the day. Storytelling is a key part of what makes us human and we are all natural storytellers. We hear stories, we tell stories, we live stories; stories are everywhere.

Story is not just the way in which we understand the world, it is the way in which we understand – and even construct – ourselves. In the same way that, when we read fiction, we create a model of the writer's imagined story world inside our head, our storytelling brain builds us a model that corresponds to our own life story. 'In order for you to tell the story of your life', writes Will Storr, author of *The Science of Storytelling*, 'your brain needs to conjure up a world for you to live inside.'[1] Our brains take disorder and convert it into narrative; they simplify and order life's muddle into a linear story. We experience external reality in relation to ourselves and to this ongoing story. We see the world, and our place in it, through the lens of our own particular life story. In her 2011 *School of Life* lecture (*On Storytelling*), neurologist Professor Susan Greenfield makes it clear that we each have a completely individual perspective on the world, which gives us our personal identity. Every life has an unrepeatable trajectory – a unique life story. Our brains are moulded by what happens to and around us, with connections between brain cells physically forming in response to our specific experiences, thus building a mind that makes us who we are. Every one of us is different but we are each, she says, living out a story. This, our life story, can give us the meaning and significance which we, as humans, seek.[2]

When I was a child, my Canadian aunt made me a patchwork quilt. Squares of the softest ditsy floral print cotton were backed with dusky pink – at the time, my favourite colour. I loved this quilt and kept it always on my bed; it was my cat's favourite place to curl up. On the days that a winter draught came through the rattly sash window in my bedroom, I would wrap the little quilt around my shoulders. On cold days, it warmed me. On sad days, it comforted me. When I grew up and left home, I took the quilt, although by this time the colour was faded and the squares were torn in places, with the wadding spilling out. I didn't mind. Its imperfections spoke to me of love. Many years later, for my godson's christening, I knew that I needed a special gift. I remembered my patchwork quilt and decided to sew one for him. Although I could use a sewing machine, I had never made a quilt

STORYTELLING IS A KEY PART
OF WHAT MAKES US HUMAN
AND WE ARE ALL NATURAL
STORYTELLERS.

*before. I bought a book and taught myself patchwork.
It was a slow and laborious process, from the selection of
the fabrics to the final hand-quilting. I felt deeply proud
of the finished result – there was love in every stitch.
This christening quilt was the first and so far the only
patchwork quilt that I made, but one day, I plan to
make another.*

*In the corner of my office, a mid-century oak sewing box
stands on long legs. I spotted it one morning in a charity
shop window, bought it and carried it home on top of a
pushchair, precariously balanced with my then-toddler
son. In this box, I collect the material for my future
quilt: pieces of fabric, each with a story to tell. There are
offcuts of the cornflower-blue Liberty-print fabric used
by my mother-in-law to make my bridesmaid's dresses,
remnants of pale cotton from clearing out my Yorkshire
granny's cupboards, scraps from cushion covers and
pieces of torn old blouses. When the time comes for me to
sew the squares together, I will also be pulling together the
stories. Alone, one little cotton square is insubstantial, but
many squares become a strong quilt, stitched together with
love, comforting and warm. A patchwork of stories is the
same; combined, arranged in a pattern that makes sense,
a patchwork of stories can begin to represent, and to find
meaning in, a life.*

Living – and telling – the stories of our lives is an ongoing quest for
meaning. We look for patterns within events as we attempt to make
sense of what author and story consultant Robert McKee terms 'the
anarchy of existence'.[3] We each seek to discover who it is that we
are and to find our own role in the world. Our life stories are the
way in which we create structure from chaos, ascribing personal
significance to the moments and events that we believe make us
who we are. A life story is a personal history, but it is also a personal
identity; in crafting this, we attempt to fathom our self and our
purpose. We communicate through the sharing of stories, both from

our own lives and from the lives of others. Stories allow us to learn, to encourage, to inspire and to effect change.

In the simplest of terms, a story – whether fictional or from life – can be reduced to the understanding that somewhere, sometime, something changed. Often, this moment of change is an event that happens to the protagonist (the leading character in the story, who – if this is a little story from your life – may well be you). The change can be subtle, though; it could be an inner change, a shift in mindset or understanding. A conceptual or emotional adjustment can influence the protagonist, but it may also occur for the story's reader. Any impactful story will open the reader's eyes to new feelings or possibilities, altering their comprehension. When we tell our own little stories, whether with words or images, we are always communicating these same three elements: somewhere (the setting or location where the story takes place), sometime (when the story takes place), something changed (the event or shift that is at the heart of the story). In our smallest stories, the element of change may also be small – a thought, an observed sensation, a tiny happening – but even little changes can be meaningful, and change represents a shift, a movement, often a kind of hope.

Stories, as we all know, traditionally have a beginning, a middle and an end. In our little stories, these elements are condensed. Each little story we choose to tell is a short episode from the larger, overarching story, the story of our life. When we tell part of our life story, how do we choose the best moment to begin? There will always be layers of moments that come before. Our little stories are cumulative and ongoing; in a sense, they neither begin nor end. The stuff of story, Rebecca Solnit writes, 'is just a cup of water scooped from the sea and poured back into it'.4 Time moves differently in the world of story – it is concentrated and not always clearly linear. When we choose the moment for a little story to begin, we can look for the causal origins of change (the events that explain why the change took place) or we can jump straight in and begin at the little story's core, with the change itself.

Learning from Flash Fiction

Flash Fiction (also known as Micro Fiction) is a genre of fiction that can be defined as a very short story. Word counts vary, but they tend to be between around 150 and 1000 words. Essentially, Flash Fiction is the fictional equivalent of our little life stories. This means that techniques inspired by the writing of Flash Fiction can be adapted to writing little stories of your life. Here are some to consider:

- Dive straight in: try to begin in the middle of your story. Don't make introductions, or set the scene. Start your story with the key event or the moment of change.

- Let your voice shine: with a little story, narrative voice is key. Your voice should pull the reader immediately into your story, making them want to find out what happened, and to hear more from you. If you want to make your voice sound warm, write as if you were speaking to someone you know and trust.

- Use precise imagery: in a little story there isn't space for lengthy explanations of events, or for protracted descriptions. Try to use imagery that shows the reader, in a brief phrase or sentence, exactly what it is that you are describing. Choose your words precisely.

- Focus on one feeling: little stories don't have space for a complex emotional landscape. Choose one feeling as the focus for your little story. This may be the emotion that you felt, or the emotion that you wish to evoke in the reader. Similarly, if you incorporate sense impressions into your story, select one sense to focus on.

- Let your words resonate: just as the first line of a story is important because it establishes your voice, the last line is similarly important because these are the words that will echo on with the reader. Try to write a final sentence that leaves the reader musing.

In your journal, use the above tips to write a little story of your life, from the present or from your past.

Using Composition to Tell Your Visual Story

When you look through the viewfinder of a camera, or the camera screen of a phone, you are composing an image. You are choosing what you wish to capture and where to place it within the frame. In doing so, you guide the viewer's eye, showing it where within the image to rest. If you make these choices consciously and reflectively, you can create an impactful image that tells a specific story.

We can use some rules of photographic composition as tools with which to tell visual stories.

- THE RULE OF THIRDS
  Imagine that your image is divided into nine equal segments (by two vertical and two horizontal lines). The rule of thirds says that the eye is naturally drawn to the points where these lines intersect and, therefore, that you should position the most important elements in your scene either along these lines or at the points of intersection. As our eyes tend to look from left to right, it can be helpful to place your subject on the right-hand line of the grid, thus ensuring that the viewer's gaze moves through the image, viewing different elements of the story before coming to rest on the main subject.

- LEADING LINES
  Looking at a photograph, our eye is naturally drawn along lines within the scene (such as walls, fences or roads). Known as leading lines, these pull us into the picture, directing our gaze towards the subject. As a storyteller, you can use leading lines to guide the viewer on a journey through the scene.

- FILL THE FRAME
  In a close-up image, the camera comes near to the subject (either through camera position or by zooming in) and it fills the frame of the photograph, with little background visible. Many camera phones now have a 'portrait' or 'close-up' mode which achieves this effect. This type of image can feel intense, pulling your viewer

directly into your story in an intimate way. It also allows you to convey the story of specific visual details.

- NEGATIVE SPACE
  The opposite of a 'fill the frame' image, an image with negative space is one in which there is considerable empty space around the subject of your photograph. Including negative space in your image defines and emphasizes the subject, drawing attention to it, whilst providing the viewer's eyes with a place to rest. The result can be a visually soothing, balanced image. In storytelling terms, negative space can be used to give a sense of scale and to pull the viewer deep into the image, as if travelling through physical space to reach the subject.

- FRAMING
  The act of framing is central to the photographer's art. When composing an image, you can look for natural frames: a window, the branch of a tree, an archway. Placing such a frame around the edges of a photograph naturally draws the eye to the focus of your story. Frames can add interest or mystery to a story, but the most obvious framing is not always the best way to tell a story. Take a moment to consider what happens if you stop to re-frame your image, looking beyond what initially caught your eye. The most interesting story may not be at the centre of the scene – it may hide, unnoticed on the edge of the picture. Changing the framing just a little can tell a new story.

- BEYOND THE FRAME
  What is beyond the frame can be just as important as what's included within it. For example, a portrait of a person whose gaze is fixed on a point beyond the image's edges; a road that winds away out of shot; an object that is only partially captured within the frame. Elements such as these allow you to hint at a story that is wider than the confines of your photograph and to encourage the viewer to engage their imagination in considering what lies beyond.

Compose a photograph that tells a story, using one or more of these photographic composition techniques. Think about what emotion or meaning you hope your story will evoke in the viewer. Then, combine a number of images into a short photo essay (a sequential collection of photographs) that tells different elements of the same story.

CHANGING THE FRAMING JUST A
LITTLE CAN TELL A NEW STORY.

There is a dynamic relationship between storyteller and audience. When we tell our little story to others, we reach out to them, offering them something of ourselves. They offer, in exchange, their active participation in the story: they use their imaginations to bring it to life. The audience builds the world of our story in their own minds, adding colour, texture and light. In the same way, the audience of a visual story will imagine reasons for, or scenes that occur beyond the images. As storytellers, the feedback that we receive from our audience – whether it comes in the form of eye contact and body language as we relate a tale to a friend, or the comments on a social media post that we have shared – allows us to fine-tune our storytelling and to re-shape our narratives.

When we read a story, or view a photograph, we take an imaginative leap and enter into it. We insinuate ourselves into the empty spaces, we put ourselves in the place of the protagonist or the photographer and we see the world – albeit briefly – from their point of view. This is the experience that an audience seeks from our stories. We need to guide them gently, leaving sufficient space in the story for them to engage with our world and to step in. As storytellers, we seek to capture and hold audience attention. The stories that we choose to tell reveal us, both to others and to ourselves. Attention is central to the processes of story and commanding attention may be one of the evolutionary reasons why we tell stories. Professor Brian Boyd, author of *On the Origins of Stories*, notes that in social animals, the ability to command the attention of the group confers status on an individual, which tends to give them priority access to resources and, therefore, offers them a higher chance of survival.[6] And, as with Scheherazade and the tales of *One Thousand and One Nights*, having the skill to hold the attention of an audience by telling compelling stories could once have meant the difference between life and death. For us, the stakes are nowhere near so high. Nevertheless, in the same way that we recognize the intrinsic value of our own attention, we should recognize that the attention of others is also precious. If we want to attract and hold the attention of an audience, our little stories must offer them something worthwhile in return.

The remarkable human ability to imagine, predict and interpret the behaviour of other people is referred to by psychologists as 'theory of mind', a capability which is essential for storytelling. By enabling us to consider and explore the viewpoints of others, stories use and develop our capacity for empathy. This is what allows us to journey into their imaginative realm and it is what builds the connection between storyteller and audience. We may find ourselves naturally drawn to storytellers with similar backgrounds or frames of reference to our own, because the details and associations within their stories will feel familiar and comprehensible. But story also enables us to connect with those whose lived experiences differ from ours. It offers us the chance to empathize and connect with people from all backgrounds and viewpoints. Stories, says Diana Evans, 'show us back to ourselves and open windows onto other pictures, other lives'.[7] If, as we share our own little stories, we make the choice to seek out and engage with those from a diverse range of fellow storytellers, stories can foster empathy and bring us together. 'The magic of story', writes Will Storr, 'is its ability to connect mind with mind in a manner that's unrivalled even by love.'[8]

Story is a force for good, but stories can be used in order to control or oppress. The expression 'control the narrative' refers to consciously manipulating the way in which the story of a particular event, person or situation is portrayed. In her 2009 TED Talk 'The Danger of a Single Story', author Chimamanda Ngozi Adichie explains that stories are tied up with power, which she refers to as 'the ability not just to tell the story of another person, but to make it the definitive story of that person'. Reducing a person, or people, to one single story is dangerous and damaging: it creates stereotypes and emphasizes differences. Adichie argues that stories should instead be used to 'empower and to humanize'. She says that 'many stories matter'; people are multifaceted and each of us is composed of many varied stories.[9] Connecting with others, and recognizing their whole and equal humanity, involves engaging with the multiple differing stories that make them who they are, whilst contributing a full range of stories that make us who we are. The opportunity to share your story in your own voice is in itself a form of freedom and privilege. Storytelling space needs to be to be opened up to all. It's important that – as we tell our own stories – we also take the time to listen to and (if we can) share the voices of others, particularly those whose stories are not being widely heard.

There is always more than one possible way to tell and interpret any given story, and a question we should ask – of the stories we tell and the stories we hear – is 'why is this particular story, told in this particular way?' Truth (not manipulation or control) is what should be at a story's heart. Every story has a significance or an underlying message – whether intentional or not and, as students of literature know, stories can have multiple possible meanings, with hidden depths and varied interpretations. Memoir, like fiction, is a literary form and our own little stories resemble snippets of memoir, which is to say that they are narrative writing based on our personal memories. But a memoir is more than a straightforward, factual retelling of events. As storytellers, we can learn from the craft of memoir that simply telling the reader what happened is not always enough. A writer of memoir reflects back on their experience across the distance of time, with the benefit of hindsight to lend nuance. In doing so they can learn from, and make a kind of sense of, events of their past. They can convey this on the page by writing in what is called the reflective voice. Sentences may begin with phrases such as 'I believed', 'I learned', I realized', 'I used to think' or 'I came to understand'. This is a writing technique that we can adopt in our own storytelling. Making use of the reflective voice when you tell your own little stories will clarify and expand your personal narrative voice. Sharing your interpretation of events will invite the reader to feel closer to you. The reflective voice is a technique that allows us to interpret events from a considered perspective, to understand the meaning behind them and to make these interpretations explicit to the reader and to ourselves.

WHEN WE READ A STORY,
OR VIEW A PHOTOGRAPH, WE
TAKE AN IMAGINATIVE LEAP
AND ENTER INTO IT.

Practise Writing in the Reflective Voice

- Compose a short account of a little story from your life. Write down what happened in the simplest way you can.

- Re-write the same story, telling it reflectively from the point view of experience. Consider what you know now that you didn't know at the time the story took place. What connections are clear to you in retrospect? What reasons can you see for the events that took place? What were the consequences of these events? What have you learned from them? What have you done differently as a result? As you tell the story, you are now writing from a position of understanding, perhaps even wisdom. Can you interpret the events that took place in a way that offers insight to the reader and to yourself?

- Re-read both versions of the story. How do they differ? Are there any elements of this voice of reflection that you could replicate in your future little stories?

Infusing events with insight by writing in the reflective voice gives a story greater depth and a more overt meaning. It reveals more of the truth at the story's heart. In telling our own little stories, the change that propels every story will reveal something to us. Change may be represented by a choice that we have made, a lesson we have learned, a sensation we have felt or a conflict that we have overcome. If we take a reflective approach to our own storytelling, we consider not only what the change is, but also what that change has taught us. Understanding the significance of some of the little stories of your life can take you a step closer to understanding the significance of your life as a whole. We question our stories and our stories in turn ask questions of us. The whispered query at the centre of every little story is 'who am I?'. We tell our stories in order to make sense of our lives, but we also tell them to make sense of ourselves. Stories help us to understand our particular place in existence and to navigate the distance between the outer world and our inner self. A story (whether composed of words or images) is a medium through which we can explore our decisions and motivations and crystallize our interpretation of a particular moment or event. The stories that we choose to tell, and our process of telling them, reveal us. The narrative journey of every story may come down to the protagonist's search for self, but in telling our own stories this journey becomes intensely personal. Our stories may be little, but they have strength and immediacy; they tell us something of who we really are.

Humans are endlessly fascinated by stories. We consume, analyse, dissect and attempt to manipulate and explain them. Yet stories remain hard to pin down and quantify; their essence is somehow unfathomable. The power of story surrounds us always, like a soft glowing haze. Stories are everywhere; all that we say and do is touched by story. It compels and often delights us, we are drawn to it and regularly immerse ourselves in it, but we still do not entirely understand it. Story remains thrillingly unknowable, possessed of an inexplicable enchantment. Telling our little stories is a way to tune in to this mysterious power and to begin to harness it in our own lives.

Interview with Bobette Buster

I interviewed Bobette Buster, who is a writer, producer, consultant, lecturer, screenwriter, author and story guru. She spoke to me via video call from her home in Los Angeles and was extremely generous in sharing her wisdom. Having read and loved Bobette's books (*Do Story* and *Do Listen*) I was keen to find out more about her thoughtful and insightful approach to storytelling. Here is our conversation:

Do you think that our stories can reflect us, showing us something of ourselves that we didn't see before?

I've observed that our stories are telling *us*. Who we are. When we think about storytelling, we think we're going outwards, but if you're really listening – *why* are you telling that story? People reveal themselves.

I think we live on the surface in life. We're just all skating by, trying to get from one thing to the next, but there is a vast undercurrent and it's really trying to reach up to us and bring us into full consciousness. I've always found in my storytelling workshops that people hadn't really listened at first to what their story was telling them. Telling your story leads you on an inner journey, I see it time and time again.

Can you tell me a little about what you call the 'gleaming detail'?

In my book I use this term *gleaming detail*… it's an Irish term. In one detail you get the whole world. I've never seen it to fail. Everyone who tells a story fashions or hooks the story on one detail. It could be a smell, could be a sound, or a taste memory. Certain people are very tactile when they describe something; we all have one sense that we're more orientated to. I love hearing other people's stories, particularly if we went through the same experience (whatever it may be) – they're always going to reflect a different dimension of it. I think that when you slow down and allow yourself to experience the moment, whatever attracts you – you magnify your attention on it. That's what creates a connection with other people.

You talk about observing the extraordinary in the ordinary. Do you think that the key to finding it is stopping, listening and taking time to notice things?

I think it truly is the meditation of life to slow down and be present in the moment, and every day presents something beautiful. We all live such stressful lives, we're always multi-tasking, in our heads and elsewhere – we're impatient. Every day is shouting at us to stop and take notice and then we will be restored. I think that we are continually being called to restoration, to pause.

I remember once being at Haight-Ashbury, a busy street in San Francisco. Creeping across the street was a large caterpillar with a gold stripe down its back. It could have been crushed any minute, so I stopped and scooped it up and put it in the grass of a park. My friends laughed at me, but when I went home, I looked it up and that caterpillar would have become a huge moth with extraordinary markings. I just dared to stop in my tracks and interface with a creature.

We're constantly being given opportunities to have a multi-dimensional life. Life is mostly whispering at you, tapping on your shoulder, sometimes shouting at you. There are different sensory levels of experience and we have forced ourselves into a narrow bandwidth. That's why we have to slow down, because we're actually living in a terribly narrow dimension. Our little stories magnify our ability to expand – even if just for a moment – a larger dimension of life that's going on.

You're asking people to pay attention to the details. In the details, story really flourishes. In movies, you cut to close-ups. You take certain details and magnify them so the audience sees them. You plant these details in what I call *rhymes* throughout the story and these *rhymes* develop emotional meaning.

I was wondering what you would say to someone who felt that their own story wasn't worth telling?

My belief is that every single person has a story to tell and that if you tell it, it's for the common good – it advances the common good. The history of storytelling is that the people who write history are telling *a* story and they're wagging their finger at everyone else saying 'Don't you dare tell *your* story'.

When people say 'I don't have a story to tell, why would anyone care?'… once you shine a light on your perception, somebody will care. I promise you. Somebody will care. It might not be in your inner circle, it might not be in your community, but that's why social media is so brilliant.

What's your advice for storytelling on social media?

I talk about this in my TED Talk, *The Radical Act of Storytelling*. I think there's a skill and a craft to storytelling. Some people are naturals at it, but most people can learn it. In my book (*Do Story*) I have the Ten Principles of Storytelling. There is a structure to storytelling that's time-based: you have to think of the rhythm of music.

If you really want to communicate, you have to be crisp and succinct, and there's a craft to be learned to do that and do it well. If you want to communicate to me something that's remarkable to you, you have to think about how you want to grab my attention.

Part of the reason that I'm interested in storytelling is its connection to family – the idea that we learn from the stories of the previous generation and pass on our own stories to the next. What do you feel is the importance of preserving stories for the future?

That's something close to my heart. My great fortune was that I came from a storytelling community. We gathered together, we took time with each other, we were respectful to our elders and we listened to them. The way they told their stories was absolutely compelling. When people you love and know have endured real hardships and big world events but survived and thrived, it creates a strengthening within you as you envision yourself doing the same. The ordinary stories are where the extraordinary moments happen. That's the fabric of life.

How can we as storytellers connect with our audience?

I think we should never underestimate the power of personal passion. What ultimately connects with people is the spark of joy that you have. You might not think you would be interested in someone else's passion, but how they talk about it – the gleam in their eye, the details, the joy that they take in arcane aspects of whatever their passion is … as you listen you become a better person. You are connecting with them through imagination and they are making you see an experience – a world – you would otherwise never have known. Sharing in their love for their passion creates communality; it's a unique moment for you both. When you listen to someone's story and lean in to their passions, you knit your emotions together with theirs.

Storytelling creates community – you're handing the baton from one person to the next, from one generation to the next:

'Take notice, I'm giving you something. Here is a wonderful thing'.

Crafting Little Stories

A story doesn't have to be dramatic to be powerful.

Story's enchantment does not exclusively reside in intricately plotted novels or epic movies. Small stories – your small stories – can also contain the same mysterious power. The enchantment begins, as the story does, at the beginning. In telling a story about yourself, you immediately open up a window into your life and invite your audience to peek inside. Whether this audience is a friend, your future self or your social media followers, your story is an invitation, a glimpse of what it means to be you. A story is a mysterious portal that creates a connection between the mind of the storyteller and the mind (or minds) of the audience. It is story's ability to connect us with others in this way that makes it so powerful. We can harness the power of story through the telling of our own stories, the little stories of our lives.

Imagine that you are meeting someone for the first time. How would you choose the first story that you tell about yourself – the story that best represents who you are? There is no correct answer to this question and, of course, your choice of story would vary according to who you were meeting and the context in which you met. There are, we know, certain core life stories that we tell over and over again. We are naturally adept at picking these stories up again from the last time that they were told, and at perfecting their nuances for the particular moment in which we are currently re-telling them. We intuitively know how to tell stories – we have been doing it all our lives – but if we want to engage more consciously with our own storytelling process, we can ask ourselves the classic information-gathering questions:

Who am I telling my story to?
What story am I telling?
Why have I chosen this story?
Where and when is my story set?
How should I set about telling my story?

The first of these questions reflects upon the intended audience for your little story. If you are recording your story in a journal, your intended audience may well be your future self, or perhaps one day those closest to you. When you tell a story to yourself, you will be your own reader and can freely reveal your innermost thoughts. You can tell each story in whatever way feels true to you in the moment and you may wish to include a level of close detail that will allow you, in the future, to recall the fabric of your life exactly as it is today. If you are sharing your story, for example, on social media, your audience will be wider. You may have a relatively private audience of friends and family, or be telling your story publicly. If you use social media for your small business, your audience will be your customers, present and future. Having a wider audience doesn't mean that you shouldn't tell stories in your own voice, but rather that you should make conscious decisions about how much of yourself and your life you feel comfortable revealing. It's also helpful to consider which of your little stories would be most likely to intrigue your audience, encouraging them to engage and to return. All these audiences are equally valid, but it's sensible to keep your intended audience in mind and to modify your tone accordingly. Storytelling is a mode of communication and your storytelling style and subject matter will vary according to who it is that you are communicating with.

What story you choose to tell will be influenced by the audience to whom you are telling it and also by the context in which your story is told. A story transcribed in your journal is likely to be more personal and reflective than a story sent to your family in an email. A story shared on social media always carries the awareness that words and images posted in the public domain can never be fully retracted. We all have different comfort levels for the degree to which we are willing to open up online. I believe that it is possible to maintain a careful degree of privacy without losing the authenticity of your voice. Keeping stories small can be key. Personally, I don't tend to share on social media the major events of my life or the details of my personal relationships. However, I will happily share the story of my morning walk, of a cake that I have baked or a place I have visited. When I tell these stories, I describe not just the experience itself, but also my feelings about it. The level of vulnerability that surfaces in storytelling will be different for everyone but it doesn't have to mean baring all and revealing your secrets; meaning can come from allowing the reader an insight into the moments that light you up. If a story means something to you, you can make it mean something to your audience – the intensity of your feeling will carry them along with you. Choose little stories that are emotionally resonant by looking for moments that contain potency of meaning or a sense of inner luminosity, moments that light you up.

If you reflect upon your reasons for choosing the story that you have chosen to tell, you will gain an insight into what that story means to you. For example, here is a little story of mine from a couple of summers ago:

Summer mist – so rare, so transient, so cool and sweetly soothing. I was drying my hair when my husband opened the curtains and called to me: 'There's mist up in the woods!' A message from a friend pinged me the same: 'Have you seen those woods?' With a little time to spare before school, the children and I took a detour. They ran along the paths calling 'This way Mum, there's fog this way!' whilst I quickly snapped pictures, feeling the silvery air like balm on my skin. Aware of the clock ticking, we bade the trees and fields farewell and hurried away to the school gates, carrying the morning calm with us like a charm for the day ahead.

I choose to tell this particular story because I wanted to record and preserve the brief wonder of that moment. I wrote it down that same day and shared it on Instagram with a photograph of the woods from the morning. My children were in school by then and the fleeting mist had faded. It was my eldest son's last summer of primary school and I knew that future mornings would be different for us, with impromptu adventures no longer an option. I wanted to hang on to our sense of freedom for as long as I could. This little story was a bookmark of sorts – a memory marker to return to. To my audience, I hoped to communicate the essence of the experience and to my husband and my friend (both of whom know my love of photographing the mist), I wanted to communicate that I appreciated them for making the adventure possible by thinking of me. Most of all, I was recording all of this for my future self. I knew that the photographs I had taken that morning would remind me of the moment, but I combined them with words so that I would be sure to recall how the mist felt on my skin, and my children's shared enthusiasm in the instant, the echo of their voices amongst the trees. To me, this smallest of stories means something far loftier than the story itself. It represents freedom, beauty, friendship and love.

The fourth of our questions (When and where is the story set?) considers the context; in storytelling, context is key. Remember that any story can be condensed down to 'somewhere, sometime, something changed'. Two out of these three elements are the context. Your audience needs to know when the story is set ('sometime') and where it takes place ('somewhere'). You don't have to adopt the 'once upon a time' approach and tell this explicitly, you can include clues that show when and where the story occurs. In my little story above, we know that it takes place on a summer morning. I mention the season in the first sentence (to establish the rarity of the mist). The time of day can be extrapolated from the fact that I was drying my hair (typically a morning activity), coupled with the fact that the action takes place 'before school'. Then, in the final line, I confirm this when I write about the 'morning calm'. The location of the story begins at home ('I was drying my hair when my husband opened the curtains'), moves to the woods and finally ends at the school gates. The *change* in this story is facilitated by the weather (unexpected mist), which transforms an ordinary morning into an impromptu adventure. In order for an audience to engage with your story, it should be rooted in a time and a place. You don't need lengthy descriptions to establish this, just a few carefully chosen words. If you're unsure as to whether your story has context, re-read it and check that it would be clear to the reader when (the time of day, season or point in your life) and where (the location) it took place.

Asking yourself how you should set about telling the story is an opportunity to consider some techniques that can be helpful when telling your little stories. As we have established, a story originates from a moment of change, whether external (an event or happening) or inner (a shift in mindset or feeling). This change can take the form – as in my story above – of an experience or revelation, but it can also take the form of conflict. Fictional stories typically contain some form of conflict, usually between the protagonist and another character, society or even nature. Although it's possible that our own small stories will involve conflict with someone else, conflict in a small story is more likely to be internal: the tension between the contrasting elements of ourselves. We may also find ourselves in conflict with nature if our small story contains some kind of everyday struggle, such as getting caught in the rain. Sometimes, I find that as I write a little story, the nature of the change is not clear to me at first. This can be because the change is occurring within me and it's not until I return later to the story that its deeper meaning becomes apparent.

When I was eighteen years old, I left home and got on an aeroplane to spend a year teaching English in a school in Thailand. I carried with me nothing more than I could squeeze into a single twenty-kilogram rucksack. Every item earned its place in my luggage – clothes, shampoo, malaria tablets, my camera and an A4 hardback notebook, pages empty, its cover meticulously covered in a rainbow patchwork of pictures. That notebook was my diary and I wrote in it without fail every single day of my trip, moving on when the pages were complete to notebook after notebook, each with a new patchwork cover, pages swiftly filled to bursting with my enthusiastic scrawl.

Back then, I didn't have such a thing as an email account, let alone social media – it was just me, my camera, my pen and page after page of blank paper. The words flowed out of me on humid evenings in the room I shared with my dear friend Annie. We sat writing together, cross-legged on the wooden floor, each attempting to capture in our own way the wonder of those wide-eyed days. At the end of the year, my stack of diaries (too heavy now for the battered rucksack) were boxed up and made their way to England by sea, my year's story entrusted to the postal service. When I arrived home, I found the box on my bedroom floor, dented and scrawled, but intact.

Flicking through my diary years later I read just a couple of sentences:

The air hangs heavy and honey-coloured, softening the edges of everything. My bike wheels whizz in the silence.

I am instantly reminded of a long quiet road, dry and jasmine-scented, flanked by an ancient ruined temple, on the outskirts of a small Thai town. A road that I cycled down every day of my nineteenth year. I think about how it feels to become so infused with the spirit of a place that, decades later, it still echoes in your dreams. I recall those seemingly endless exploratory days, in which the quotidian and the magical felt utterly entwined, and I am grateful to the girl I was then for taking the time to preserve her little stories with words, like insects suspended in amber, for me to pick up and re-live half a lifetime later.

The bones of even the smallest story are a beginning, a middle and an end. As we learned in Chapter Seven, a small story doesn't allow for lengthy beginnings. A sentence or two at the most to set the context, a little story should pull the reader straight in to the key event or moment of change. The middle of a little story needs to maintain this momentum, weaving the events of the story together and drawing the story's action to a close. This leaves space at the end of the little story: an opportunity for reflection on its meaning or emotional significance. The final sentences can be used to hint at the effect that has been created by the change at the heart of the story – the way in which the world, or you the storyteller, are different. One satisfying way for a story to conclude is for the ending to contain an echo of the story's beginning, whether through context, event, image or word choice. Even a small story can accommodate a recurring motif – an image or idea that is repeated through the course of the story. A simple way to achieve this is by electing for the end of the story to reflect, in some way, the beginning. This satisfies our natural human inclination towards pattern and it also highlights the story's crucial aspect of change; although the story is cyclical, and we return to the beginning, something – often we ourselves – has been altered by the journey.

Although the smallest of stories have a basic narrative framework, little stories can borrow from poetry as much as from prose. Like a poem, a little story encapsulates a feeling or experience using a minimal number of words. This is an immediate, concentrated form of storytelling. The little stories of our lives don't conform to a plot, they are brief and often impressionistic: a record of thoughts, occurrences and senses. In a little story, images can be tumbled together, using descriptive words that have an immediacy to draw the audience in. There will be a written structure, but there can also be gaps, hints and unanswered questions. Transcribing our little stories in a journal first allows us to write with a sense of freedom and to experiment freely with words. There is no wrong way to tell your little stories, because they belong to you. The best inspiration for writing is always to read and poetry has much to offer the storyteller. If you don't usually read poetry, why not consider opening up a poetry book or finding a poem online. Like a poem, a little story can have different layers of meaning. There is a simple, surface meaning, but in addition there may be a deeper meaning. This deeper meaning is what the little story tells you about who you are. It can also encompass a sense of universality, allowing other people to identify with your little story and to take something from it that resonates with their own experience.

Humans respond positively to pattern in storytelling – repeated elements, a return to the beginning or a predictable form – but we also respond to contrast. Juxtaposition is a technique used by artists of all genres. It consists of placing paired elements side by side to highlight their differences and create contrast. In storytelling terms, this means bringing together two disparate ideas or elements. The interplay between the two will enliven the story. In a written story you can juxtapose settings (such as indoors and outdoors), character traits (such as kindness and selfishness), images (such as a new hat with an old, dented hat) or concepts (such as freedom and confinement). Juxtaposition isn't usually overt – you don't need to actively explain it to the reader, but you can weave the

THE BONES OF EVEN THE
SMALLEST STORY ARE A
BEGINNING, A MIDDLE
AND AN END.

two different entities into your story and let the comparison occur naturally. Juxtaposition can also be a particularly effective visual storytelling tool. Take some time to explore creative ideas and play with juxtaposition in photography. For example, juxtaposing natural objects with a man-made setting (or vice versa), curves with straight lines; old with new, large with small. You'll find ideas for creative juxtaposition in visual storytelling in the Photography Exercise in Chapter Four. My own experience has been that my audience always engage particularly well with images that use juxtaposition to tell a story. Juxtaposition intrigues us, causing us to stop and take notice – to engage our imagination, to look again. It's an effective way to make your images stand out in a crowded social media feed.

The five questions that we posed at the start of the chapter are as applicable to storytelling with images as they are to storytelling with words. When you compose a photograph (or a series of photographs) in order to tell a story, consider exactly what story you are telling, why you are telling it and who your audience is. Context is important in visual storytelling, too – it is represented to the viewer through visual clues that establish the location, as well as the time of day and time of year. In a photograph, varied elements of story can exist in the form of details and visual layers. Visual layers are created by the different parts of the image: the foreground (up close, at the front of the image), the mid-ground (in between foreground and background) and the background (further away in the distance, at the back of the image). Details, as we have considered, lend meaning and specificity. Sometimes, the composition of a storytelling image will lead the viewer's eye on a journey within the frame, moving from layer to layer or detail to detail, guided by the positioning of objects or leading lines within the image. In other images, particularly those that utilize negative space, the story may be immediately clear and visually arresting.

Telling a Still-Life Story

Sometimes, a scene appears before us, ready to be a captured, but on other occasions we may wish to create an image by arranging or observing a still-life scene that tells the story of a particular moment. Visual storytelling is a practice that combines the rules of composition with styling skills and creativity to compose still-life images that tell a specific story. Whether creating intricate flatlay scenes (objects on a surface photographed from above), like those on social media or in magazines, or merely tweaking the tiniest of details before snapping an everyday vignette, an understanding of the elements of visual storytelling can help us to create images that tell a still-life story

Seek inspiration from still-life paintings and the way in which artists capture a scene. You are the artist here. You have the freedom to create in your own way and to tell a story using your unique visual voice. Unlike a candid photograph of a spontaneous moment, when shooting a still-life image you can take your time. Think about how to tell the story of this moment and plan your image before you shoot it.

- Begin with the light. Consider its source, strength and direction. When you position objects in the scene, do so with the light in mind. Use it to direct the mood.

- Consider which are the key objects in the image. Remember the rule of odds – you may wish to have one main object and a couple of subordinate objects. Each element you include should tell part of the story.

- Consider framing. You may wish to work from the outside in, placing objects in such a way that they lead the eye into the scene.

- Consider balance. Where in the frame are objects positioned? Make your story flow by encouraging the viewer's eye to move actively around the scene.

- Think beyond the frame – use glimpses and hints to imply what is happening beyond the confines of the frame, or add evidence of what took place moments before the photograph was taken (such as broken eggshells from cracking an egg to make a cake).

I find that still-life images can be an impactful way to tell the story of my everyday moments, such as flowers picked from the garden, a cup of tea and a book, or a kitchen story, such as slicing vegetables or peeling fruit. Choose a still-life scene that you would like to tell the story of and experiment with composing and shooting your own still-life story.

When you compose a picture to tell the story of a moment, always ask yourself how you can establish the story's context visually and how you can indicate its meaning to the viewer. I have long been in the habit (every time I compose an image with my camera) of asking myself the question: 'What's the story here?' For me, any scene or object can potentially tell a story, but I need to understand what it is that's happening in the picture. What are the weather conditions? What is the light doing? Who has been present here? What occurred before I pressed the shutter? What will occur afterwards and why? I ask myself what this particular picture is *about*. This means recognizing what it was about the scene that drew my eye, or precisely what emotion it evokes in me (and also what emotion I hope to evoke in the viewer). Some of my pictures, although they may be taken of something visually pleasing, just don't work. In my experience this is almost always because they do not have an underlying narrative. In photography, as in life, story is everything.

One key way in which to infuse your photographs with emotion is to practise becoming aware of your own feelings as you are shooting. As we considered in Chapter Two, taking a meditative approach to photography can help us to engage more deeply with the act of taking a photograph. The camera is an instrument that records what your eye sees and – with practice – what your heart feels. Having a conscious understanding of your own state of mind can feed into the mood that you create with your picture, which will help you to tell the story of the scene. In any story (written or visual), the mood is the atmosphere or ambiance; it is the feeling that you are looking to evoke in your audience. Try to get into the habit of asking yourself 'how does this make me feel?' and then 'how can I capture this feeling through the mood of my image?' If you have an emotional connection with the story that you are telling and the mood that you are creating, it's far more likely that your image will elicit an emotional response from your audience. There are many ways in which mood can be created in an image: choice of moment, colour palette, light, angle and scale all have a part to play.

Enhancing the Mood of an Image

LIGHT
When you take a photograph, be aware of the light conditions and make use of them as best you can in order to enhance the mood of your story. For example, images shot in the golden hour (before sunset or after sunrise) will have a soft glow or (if you shoot into the light and create lens flare) an other-worldly sparkle. Images shot on a rainy day will be muted and calm (the light is dulled by the clouds) and images shot in full, bright sunlight will be saturated with colour and, depending on the direction in which you shoot, may contain shadows.

COLOUR PALETTE
The colours that you choose to include in the frame can drastically alter the mood of your image: think of the contrast between bright, primary colours and pale, natural tones. Take care to select colours that support the story that you wish to tell and the feeling that you want to evoke. The tones of an image can be tweaked using a photo editing app, but be consciously aware of the colours that you initially include in the frame.

ANGLE AND SCALE
Varying your camera position is one of the simplest ways to change the mood of an image – shooting from close up or far away, from above or below, through a frame or straight on to camera – each of these can produce varied feelings and tell a different story. To practise varying your camera angle, experiment with different ways of photographing a single object, such as a leaf. Here are some examples.

- From a distance, on the tree, small and surrounded by other leaves.

- Zoomed in with a close-up of the leaf, perhaps held in a hand.

- From above, as the leaf lies fallen on the forest floor.

- From below, glowing as the light shines through the leaf.

- Shot through the other leaves on the tree, focussed on one leaf and framing it with the others.

In your journal, note down how the story and mood of the image changes each time.

When you are telling the story of one particular day, try to anticipate the key events that will form the story and encapsulate the day. To use a commonly photographed example: at a child's birthday party, you would want to capture the birthday child blowing out the candles on their cake. By planning this in advance, you can ensure that you're ready before the time comes, that you've observed the direction of the light and positioned yourself accordingly. If you take pictures before, during and after the key instant that you anticipate, you can capture the full range of feelings that surround it. In this case it might be the anticipation on the child's face, their joy in blowing out the candles, followed by a poignant interaction as a loving parent realizes that yet another year has passed. In addition to anticipating predictable events, I love to look for the liminal moments: the in-between times when nothing important is happening, but when people are often their truest, most unguarded selves. If you are attuned to these transitional times, it's possible to capture quiet examples of connection or solitude and poignant, passing details that others may not notice. In the context of a birthday party, this might be a close up of a child's hand placing their handwritten card on the table, a toddler playing with a balloon, two friends talking and laughing, or a child in a fancy-dress costume standing on tiptoe to peek at the cake. Often, I find that these types of images become far more precious to me than the classic celebratory shots, because liminal moments tell stories that are unexpected and unique.

There are proven personal benefits to recording and telling our little stories. A 2016 study (by Kristin Diehl of the University of Southern California, Gal Zauberman of Yale University and Alixandra Barasch of the University of Pennsylvania) showed that using photography to record our positive experiences increases our enjoyment.[1] The mental process that we adopt when taking a photograph heightens our engagement with an experience, and greater engagement means greater enjoyment. It seems to me that perhaps that engagement could be seen as another way to describe

paying attention. A different study, in 2018, found that daily photography can support everyday well-being.[2] This study focused on the digital daily practice of 'photo-a-day' (taking a photograph every day and sharing it online). The authors of this study (Liz Brewster of Lancaster University and Andrew Cox of the University of Sheffield) highlighted three interlinked aspects of a 'photo-a-day' practice: self-care, community practice, and reminiscence and reflection. Each of these has the potential for improved well-being. Taking a photograph can be an act of self-care, in part because of photography's mindful nature. Sharing the same photograph online encourages interaction and engagement with others, making it an example of a positive community practice. Reminiscence and reflection occur when a photograph is used to look back at a past event, providing a reminder of the moment recorded. The 2016 study also suggested that photographs can be used beneficially in order to revisit experiences and to allow us potentially to re-live the enjoyment we felt at the time of shooting. Returning to, and reliving, happy memories is what some psychologists call 'positive reminiscence'.

It appears, therefore, that there are a number of potential advantages of using photography to tell our stories, if we record positive experiences. The act of *taking* a photograph can be beneficial because it increases engagement and encourages mindfulness. The *sharing* of a photograph allows us to connect and engage with an online community. Photographs can also be used as *aide-mémoires*, *reconnecting* us with an experience and allowing us to remember and relive the happiness that we felt at the time the image was taken. A collection of photographs – of little stories – represents a bank of memories that we can return to in order to remember good times, and feel happier as a result. But recording negative experiences also has consequences. The same 2016 study found that photo-taking has the opposite effect when the experience is negative, meaning that using photography to record unhappy experiences is likely to preserve our unhappiness – the way that we feel when a photograph is taken appears to be the way that we will feel again when we revisit it. However, when writing in a journal, the reverse has been suggested to be true: we benefit from writing about our feelings and experiences, even if our feelings are negative. Professor Matthew Lieberman writes that 'putting your feelings into words is good for you', even when those feelings are troubling or distressing.[3] His research has found that the action of labelling (writing down) our feelings changes the pattern of activity in our brains. In the short term, the result of this is that we become less distressed by things that worry or frighten us; in the long term, the result is that we become less stressed, which can contribute to better physical health. In summary, recording your feelings in your journal may make you healthier and happier, and the same is true of using photography to record (and share) positive experiences, particularly if you look back over your photographs in order to remember happy moments. Telling your little stories is not just a creative outlet, a collection of memories and a form of self-expression – it can be actively good for you.

One function of a written little story is to express feelings, but it can also exist as a sort of descriptive time capsule. Sometimes, particularly when we feel a moment deeply, we find ourselves compelled to pull it out of the flow of time, to hold it, examine it closely and attempt to commit it to memory. But a little story is not a record of the moment itself, it is a record of our *perception* of the moment. Our stories are not objective accounts – they always tell us more about ourselves than they say about events that occurred. It is through our interaction with the moment that we create meaning. When you write a descriptive time capsule that tells the story of a moment, you are recording what it was to be you – who you were at that particular instant in time. For example, here is a little story that I jotted down (initially in the notes of my phone, then later transcribed to a notebook and finally posted on my blog) on the day that my son (the youngest of my three boys) turned one:

The day he turned one, I sat with him, under a summer sky, on the cliffs of Cape Cornwall. He played amongst the swathes of pink thrift flowers, running his chubby little fingers through them, picking the occasional bloom and handing it to me, with a mischievous twinkle in his wide blue eyes. I stretched out my toes in the sunshine and marvelled at his perfect, white-golden curls. Below us, in the rock pools, his beloved brothers were seeking crabs, their excited voices carrying up to us on the warm salty air.

The day he turned one, I held him on my lap and sang 'happy birthday' to him, over and over, whilst he giggled in appreciation, holding on to my arm with his dimpled hand. We looked out to sea and I held him close, feeling the soft weight of him and the breeze against my skin and trying to imprint upon my heart a memory of the loveliness of it all.

Seven years later, my youngest is now a rapidly growing boy, but whenever I re-read these words, I am transported back to that sunny late May morning, sitting on the windswept clifftop and breathing salt air, with the weight of my little one on my lap. A photograph would (and did) record the moment, but this written description ensures that I remember in some detail how it *felt* to be me back then. A descriptive time capsule is a repository for memories that can be revisited, in the same way that we might flick through a photo album – it has the capacity to allow us to experience positive reminiscence, pulling us back into the past where we can revisit the happiness we felt.

Descriptive Time Capsules

In your journal, write your own descriptive time capsule for a happy or poignant moment that you would like to preserve in order to allow yourself to revisit it in the future. The aim here is to use written description to preserve aspects that might be lost in a photograph. Capture sensual details: record the sounds you can hear, the smells, the temperature, the quality of light and the sensations on your skin. Include any movement, however slight, in your description. Try to transcribe your experience of the moment in as much detail as you can, to allow your future self to step back into it. Don't assume that a memory of your feelings will remain with you – put them into words. The aim here is to imprint a memory in your mind and on your heart, but the time capsule exists as a way in which to jog your recollection, allowing you to return to this moment.

Sometimes, the most difficult part of storytelling is deciding what story to tell. Like digging for diamonds, we can mine for potential stories in the most mundane locations. If you're feeling uninspired, consider that everyday little stories are usually found in everyday places. Your mobile phone is almost certainly full of story inspiration. Scroll through your camera roll, choose an image that stands out for you and tell its story. Phone notes are also a brilliant source of inspiration. Sentences that have been jotted down as an *aide-mémoire* become cryptic over time. They may jog your memory and remind you of an untold story, or they can also spark a train of thought that leads to a new idea. Dig and see what you find. Alternatively, put down your phone and look around your house. Can you tell the story of your discarded shopping list, or of the birthday card folded between the pages of your book? How about the photograph propped up on the mantelpiece or the papers stuck to the fridge? Wherever there are traces of who you are, there are little stories to be told. Tell the story of your muddy boots by the front door, of the pictures that you carry in your wallet or of the vine that raps against your kitchen window. Look for a little story that tells of what it is to be you, right now, in this moment.

Over time, as you collect together your little stories, you will begin to build up a wider picture, a picture of who you are. Just as a life is made up of many, many days, all stitched together, a *life story* is made up of many, many *little stories*. When you tell little stories that reflect your passions and preoccupations, stories that communicate what's on your mind and what's in your heart, these little stories accumulate into a unique vision of daily life. Your little stories combine to create a portrait of a life – your life. You are always at the centre of your little stories – they reveal the world as seen through your eyes and as told in your voice. The little stories that you tell are *about* you and they are told *by* you. In this sense, they are all self-portraits. Sometimes, though, for our stories to truly reflect who we are, we need to be brave and reveal ourselves (if only to our journals) with an actual self-portrait. It's time for us to step into our stories.

WHEREVER THERE ARE TRACES
OF WHO YOU ARE, THERE ARE
LITTLE STORIES TO BE TOLD.

Your
Story

You are at the heart of all your little stories.

Every word you write and every picture you take records the world through your eyes. Your presence is always implied, but I believe that to make your little stories truly your own, sometimes you need to step right into the story and record not just what you see, but also who you are. It takes courage to put yourself in the frame, I know that. Creating a self-portrait (whether through photography or a written description) can make us feel deeply vulnerable. We are often our own worst critics and we are used to being judged according to appearance (and perhaps found wanting). We can be made to feel that we're not beautiful, slim or young enough to show ourselves. Conversely, taking a self-portrait may make us feel shallow, as if we are succumbing to vanity. Coming out from behind the camera and into the frame can be a terrifying prospect. A few years ago, there was no-one less keen on self-portraiture than I was and yet now some of my most treasured photographs are self-portraits. They're not always images that I share – some of them may remain unseen by anyone except myself – but they are precious moments that record the story of *my* life. The thought of stepping into your own story may fill you with trepidation, but I believe it's possible to reframe your perceptions of self-portraiture. I'd like to show you that self-portraits are an essential, even a joyous way of telling the little stories of your life.

Given that your aim is to tell the little stories of *your* life, those stories need to include you! As you record the world around you, don't be afraid to visibly take up space in it. A self-portrait is not about pouting, posing or showing off. It is a deeply personal expression of who you are at this particular point in time. Self-portraiture is a form of storytelling that allows you to record (with an image or a written description) how you feel about yourself. A self-portrait is a gift to yourself, now and in the future. You don't have to share them – not even with family – unless you choose to, but one day, you (and, if you wish, those dearest to you) will look back at them with love and see the beauty or the truth of that particular moment in your life. Self-portraits are not an expression of narcissism, they are the clearest way to record what it means to be you, right now.

Beside the desk in my office, I have a few favourite self-portraits tacked to the wall. They are the touchstones that I return to when my sense of who I am starts to drift or when my confidence is at a low ebb. There is a black-and-white film photograph that I took of myself in my late teens leaning against the wall of my parents' cottage, eyes lowered, friendship bracelets twisting around my bare arms, camera propped up on a wall. There is a blurry polaroid that I snapped recently on a Welsh beach (camera held in front of me, face too close but happy, hair wet from a swim in the sea), and there is the print of an image that I shot a decade ago with my phone, pointing the lens into the bathroom mirror at my bleary sleep-deprived eyes and tousled morning hair – newborn son asleep on my shoulder. I love these photographs not because they captured me from a good angle – in one I am out of focus and in another I look exhausted – I love them because they remind me how it felt to be me at those different points in my journey. They allow me to remember who I was and so to understand better who I am.

As with all our little stories, self-portraits have the potential to capture experiences or feelings that might otherwise be forgotten. They allow you to record your interpretation of the world in an entirely unique way. Self-portraiture is both a valuable storytelling tool and a rewarding creative process. When you shoot a photographic self-portrait (whether with a camera or with your phone), as both photographer and subject you are completely in control. You don't need to look perfect, you just need to be yourself. Self-portraits can help you to tap into your inner courage and they offer a creative opportunity to experiment. *You* have the capacity to change the angle, the lighting, the mood and the composition. You can take as many shots as you need until you get one that feels exactly right and expresses the precise story that you are looking to tell.

'Self-portraits are not innocent reflections of what artists see when they look in the mirror', notes Frances Borzello in her book *Seeing Ourselves: Women's Self-Portraits*. 'They are part of the language painters use to make a point, from the simple "this is what I look like" to the more complicated "this is what I believe in".'[1] A self-portrait is a deliberate composition that tells a specific story. When we set out to create a self-portrait, we need to consider not just *how do I look*, but, more importantly, *what do I want to say* and as ever, *what story do I wish to tell?* Whilst painting may be a traditional medium of self-portraiture, for our purposes a self-portrait is a photograph or piece of writing that you make of, or about, yourself. The aim is to be present in your own story, in a manner that feels comfortable to you. For example, by shooting our hands, feet or shadows, we can take photographic self-portraits without venturing to put our faces or whole bodies in the shot.

Self-portraiture does not have to be serious – you can be playful, explore and have fun. Sometimes, my own self-portraits are impetuous and spur-of-the-moment. I notice my shadow on a wall, I pass an interesting reflective shop window, I find a pretty patch of light on the pavement or I snap my freshly cut hair in the bathroom mirror. At other times, they are carefully thought out.

THE AIM IS TO BE PRESENT IN YOUR
OWN STORY, IN A MANNER THAT
FEELS COMFORTABLE TO YOU.

When I have an idea for an interesting self-portrait – a feeling that I want to express, a location that I'd like to capture, or even a weather condition that can be woven into the story – I make a plan, scrawling notes on a scrap piece of paper or a page of my notebook. I begin by considering *what story do I want to tell about myself?* I think about the location in which I want to take the image, what I wish to wear, the time of day most likely to give me the light conditions that I want and whether I will include any items with me in the image to add detail to the story I hope to tell. Sometimes I roughly sketch the portrait that I wish to take, although I always find that my ideas evolve as I am shooting. My planned portraits are taken with my camera (set to self-timer) and a tripod, but you could equally use your phone (set to self-timer) and a tripod, or a makeshift tripod setup, such as carefully propping your phone against a log or a windowsill.

In my self-portraits, I often play with scale. I favour images with plenty of negative space (where I am relatively small amongst a larger landscape). I first began taking images like this after a conversation with my friend, writer and photographer Julia Williams.[2] Knowing that I didn't enjoy taking photographs of myself, she suggested I tried shooting from a distance. She explained that she found it less intimidating to appear as a small figure in her images than to be close to the camera and large, filling the frame. This advice changed self-portraits for me. I felt far less self-conscious taking this kind of image and, as I began to experiment, I discovered that negative space is also a brilliant tool for storytelling. It allows me to bring the landscape that I love into my photographs and incorporate it into the stories that I tell. It shifts the focus in myself-portraits from what I look like, to what I want to say.

Utilizing the contrast between stillness and movement can make a powerful difference to self-portrait stories. When I shoot with my tripod, I take a range of varied images at the same location.

I experiment with poses: looking up, looking down, with my back to the camera, in the middle of the image, at the side, etc. I introduce movement into my images by swishing my skirt, shaking my head, walking across the frame or twirling on the spot. A still, perfectly focussed image tells a different story to a blurred, active image. The blur means that active images can seem imperfect, but motion gives a self-portrait life and infuses it with a different emotion from a static image. Framing is another way to change the story that your self-portrait tells. A mirror self-portrait (or one taken in the reflection of a window or puddle) provides a clear frame, but frames can also be found or created in a wild setting. For example, you can position your tripod so as to shoot through leaves or ferns, blurring the edges of your image, or you can use the shape of trees as a natural frame.

Taking a Self-Portrait

FEET

Perhaps the quickest and easiest way to be present in a photograph
is to point your camera or phone downwards and take a picture
of your feet. Whether it's the tips of your toes or your feet and
legs from below the knee, you literally step into the frame. By
photographing your footsteps, you record snapshots from your
ongoing journey through the world. These types of shots are a
great way to experiment with composition. Consider your use of
colour and pattern, or creating diagonal lines to give your images
dynamism. My camera roll contains countless photographs of my
feet: in a carpet of wild garlic blooms, on a flight of steps, at the
edge of the train platform. It's the simplest of way I know of saying
this is me, I am here. In the process of looking down, I notice and
record details that I would otherwise have walked straight past: the
fallen cherry blossom, the shaft of light across the pavement, the
cracked floor-tile.

HANDS

Similarly, hands – a naturally expressive part of the body – can make
for arresting images. It's possible to take an image of one of your
hands (for example, holding out an object in the foreground of your
image) by reaching out your phone or camera at a distance, but if
you wish to photograph both of your hands you will need to use a
tripod. The photographer's hand is a gentle reminder to the viewer
of their existence behind the camera. It can act as an invitation
to engage more closely with the image. By choosing to hold an
object (a book, a pen, a leaf, a photograph, a found object), you can
compose an image that tells a story about what holds significance
for you at the current time. Hands alone have a story to tell. When
I think of those I love, I can often clearly picture their hands: my
dad's, weather-beaten and freckled; the long, elegant hands of my
teenage best friend; the ink-stained, guitar-playing fingers of
my middle boy.

SHADOW

On a sunny day, consider taking a self-portrait by shooting your own shadow, against a wall or the ground. Silhouette self-portraits have an other-worldly quality – your shadow is of you and yet it is not you. Shadows don't have to feel dark; they can allow you to be present in your images in a relaxed and fun way. If I'm shooting in the summer – for example, on a day at the beach – I often include a shadow shot (inevitably along with a photograph of my toes at the edge of the waves) to ensure that I'm not constantly hidden behind the camera. A wave of a hand, a blowing scarf or a swishing skirt are all ways in which to add movement, life and interest to a shadow self-portrait.

THE SIMPLE SELFIE OR 'BACK OF THE PHONE' CAMERA

This is the quickest and easiest way to take a self-portrait. Using your phone, switch from the front-facing camera to the rear-facing camera so that your face is visible on screen and compose your shot. Like the old-school 'arm's length' self-portrait (are you old enough to remember shooting on a disposable film camera, holding it away with the lens pointing towards yourself, smiling, hoping for the best and pressing the shutter?), a selfie-style 'back of the phone' image has limited scope for composition, but it's a brilliant way to record a moment or a feeling spontaneously, to take an image that includes your own face and says *this is me, I am here.*

TRIPOD AND SELF-TIMER

Whether shooting with your phone or with your camera, a tripod allows you complete creative freedom in your self-portraits. If you shoot with a tripod, compose your image and set your camera (or phone) to self-timer mode. If you don't have a camera remote (I use an app on my phone), try to find an object that's in line with where you plan to stand, focus on that and then step into shot. If (like me) you forget your tripod or if you don't have one, you can often create a makeshift arrangement such as propping your camera or phone on a wall, log or other steady surface. Don't be afraid to utilize negative space in your images – you don't have to fill the frame, you can be further away from the camera and, therefore, smaller. When I first started taking self-portraits I felt much more comfortable composing images in which I was a small figure. When I shoot in the natural landscape, the world around me is also part of the story that I tell.

REFLECTIONS

These are my personal favourites. Less complicated than a tripod, but with more flexibility than a 'back of the phone' shot, reflective shots can be taken in mirrors, windows, puddles or any other shiny surface that creates a reflection. One of my most treasured images is that bleary-eyed mirror self-portrait taken when my youngest was a newborn. It transports me instantly back to those sleep-deprived, chaotic and euphoric days.

Photographs taken in mirrors are not the product of vanity. Frances Borzello says that they 'demand the photographer's skill at trapping and framing the image of herself'.[3] One photographer who had this particular skill was Vivian Maier, an American street photographer who took self-portraits with her Rolleiflex medium format film camera. She shot not just in mirrors, but in all manner of reflective surfaces, from shop windows to car wing mirrors. An archive of her self-portrait images can be found online and it is a fascinating source of inspiration.[4]

Your phone camera is the perfect tool for creating a reflective image of yourself. It is always to hand, so when you come across a puddle, an interesting window or a mirror, you can quickly frame a shot. I also often take self-portraits using the mirrors in my own home. I know from experience that the mirror above my bathroom sink receives the prettiest light in the house and, on the days when I want to capture an image of myself, I usually begin there.

I shoot self-portraits to capture my joys, passions and obsessions. For me, this is swimming in the sea and walking in the woods, dancing light or swirling fog. For you, it will probably be something quite different. Self-portraits reveal what lights you up and nourishes you. Think of them as a technique with which to tell the stories that matter to you most of all. As with the saltwater selfies that I described in Chapter Three, self-portraits are the most powerful tool I have to record and remember what it is to be me. When you shoot self-portraits, your gaze helps to tell the story. You can look straight into the camera, or you can turn your eyes away – looking up, down, or far into the distance. The simple movement of your eyes can change the mood and alter each portrait's story. Powerful self-portraits can be taken in moments of intensity, when your eyes are closed and your thoughts are turned inwards. The act of closing your eyes in front of the camera feels like a deliberate and powerful choice. Try to take a photo this way by setting your phone camera to rear-facing, hold it at arm's length in front of you, close your eyes, pause, then press the shutter.

Taking self-portraits should be a pleasure, not an ordeal but over time, you may find that you feel brave enough to capture the full range of your emotions – from laughter to tears. If you completed the Positive Emotions Journalling Task in Chapter Three, consider returning to it and creating a self-portrait to illustrate each of the emotions that inspired your writing. Above all, whenever you take a self-portrait be gentle with yourself and treat yourself with compassion. A self-portrait is a tender thing. In the end, although precious, the photograph that you will be left with isn't the most important part. The process itself is what has the potential to be both healing and empowering. Shooting a self-portrait is about putting yourself at the centre of your story, telling the aspects that are intimate, personal, real, or alive. It's about learning to look at yourself with acceptance and love, recognizing that your story is worth telling, that your story is everything.

Written Self-Portraits

WORD-PORTRAIT

If you are resolutely camera-shy, or if you want to combine words and images so as to record a full and complete picture of who you are at this point in your life, compose a word-portrait of yourself – a written description of who you are at this time. Whilst you can write about your physical attributes, the advantage that a written self-portrait has over a photographic one is that it allows you to map out your character, feelings and emotional attributes – elements that can only be hinted at in a photograph. You can set down something of your inner landscape and what makes you the person that you are right now. You may find the following prompts helpful:

- My face is...
- My hands are...
- I wear...
- I move like...
- I am the type of person who...
- I always...
- I never...
- The truth is that I...

ABSENT SELF-PORTRAIT

In painting, an absent self-portrait is one in which the artist paints their room or workspace, but without including themselves in the image. In portraying their personal creative space, they capture an intimate connection with their surroundings that reveals something of their inner self. The painting *A Corner of the Artist's Room in Paris* by the painter Gwen John is one effective example of an absent self-portrait. This image shows exactly what its title suggests: a window, desk and chair in the corner of the artist's room in Paris.

There is a vase of flowers on the table, an umbrella and an item of clothing draped over the chair. All that we see of Paris itself is the sloping rooftop wall and the light that streams through the window. It is a simple image, but it has a quiet intensity that leads us to imagine the story behind what we see. We wonder about the woman who carried the umbrella and who arranged the flowers. Every detail she has chosen to include is a clue.

This type of self-portrait also lends itself to written description. Think of a room, or a space within a room that belongs to you (such as a desk, shelf or mantelpiece), and experiment with writing an absent self-portrait. What clues will you include to tell a story of who you are and how you feel? In writing about your space, you describe your surroundings and the objects to be found there. You may, as in a painting, wish to leave the explanations behind the objects unsaid or, if you want to, you can include details that tell the stories behind these same objects – their origin, significance and the reason that you keep them close. You may also like to snap a photograph of the space, to accompany your words.

As an undergraduate, I wrote my dissertation on T.S. Eliot's poem *The Wasteland*. One line, from the end of the poem, has stayed with me ever since: 'These fragments I have shored against my ruins'.[5] Like all of Eliot's work, its meaning is complex and multi-layered, but to me it speaks of little stories. Our little stories are the precious fragments that we gather as we move through our days, collecting together what matters to us most of all – meaningful moments, tiny truths and everyday magic. These small shards of life may seem broken and insubstantial, but they glitter nevertheless. Gathered together, the fragments are stronger, offering support and protection against life's trials and uncertainties – guarding against the threat of collapse. A single fragment – a little story – may be delicate, but combined, they offer fortification. Your little stories are a collection of what you see, what you love and what you believe in. They are the pieces of who you are. Recording and collecting together your little stories amounts to more than simply chronicling your life; it is an act of preservation and a strengthening of self.

We are each a product both of the stories that we tell and of the tales that we are told. Family stories can help us to understand where we come from and therefore who we are. If you have children, telling them stories of personal family history can offer surprising benefits. Dr Robyn Fivush, director of the Family Narratives Lab at Emory University, has spent decades studying the beneficial effect that family stories can have on the resilience and self-confidence of children and adolescents. As part of a 2008 study that she conducted with Dr Marshall Duke[6], they developed a measure called the 'Do You Know' scale, which assessed children's knowledge of their family's stories and history through twenty questions such as 'Do you know how your parents met?' and 'Do you know which person in your family you most look like?'[7] They compared participants' answers to these questions with their results on a number of psychological tests and discovered that the more stories children knew from their own family history, the higher their self-esteem and the stronger their sense of control over their lives.[8]

'Stories', Dr Fivush wrote in a 2019 blog for *Psychology Today*, 'are naturally the way we share ourselves with each other, all the time'.[9] She views the stories that we tell our children as a 'family legacy', one which offers a host of potential benefits. Family storytelling is often an ongoing process that spans many lifetimes. From our parents and grandparents, we hear the stories of their lives and those of their own parents and grandparents. We, in turn, tell these stories to our children, adding in the stories of our own lives, which our children pass on to their children, and so the cycle continues. In sharing your stories with those you love, you also share yourself.

My Yorkshire grandad died before I was born, but for as long as I can remember, my Yorkshire granny told me stories about him. She told me the story of the day they met at a church cricket match and the story of when they married (during the war) and he asked his jeweller-friend to help him source a wedding ring for his bride (a ring that I myself now wear): 'Welsh gold, like the Queen's', my granny would say. She told me the story of the Sheffield Christmas Eve when he and a friend stayed up late, setting up a Scalextric racing car track around the Christmas tree for his sons to find the next morning; and the story of how years later, when my cousin was small, they played a game where he pretended to be a tiger so often that, in the end, he was called Grandad Tiger – by her and by all of us. I never met him, but I have always felt as if I knew him. The stories of love that kept him alive for my granny made him feel real to me.

The other side of my family is large, ever-growing and spread across the world. I am the eldest of fifteen cousins, my youngest aunt a handful of years older than me, my eldest cousins a handful of years younger. My grandma and grandad always told us stories: stories of their childhoods, their courtship and of their life with a young family of five children. Their family has grown and scattered, but stories are what bind us close.

When I am together with my cousins, we trade tales about our respective parents, the adventures of their youth and events from our shared past. At my grandad's funeral, everyone had a story to tell about what a remarkable man he was. Now, when I visit my grandma, she tells my children the familiar stories that she told to me: the story of the family guinea pigs that multiplied in number so much they had to be given to the zoo; the story of the family camping trip to Scotland when my grandad instructed his children to catch a haggis for their supper; the story of the kitten that my aunt found in the riding stables, brought home and adopted; and the story of my uncles taking shovels to the beach and building giant sand cities. My children listen spellbound, with wide eyes, just as I always did. They ask for more stories and Grandma Jean obliges, telling them stories of what took place many years ago, but also stories of now, about her other great-grandchildren who live on continents far away.

These family stories are threads that knit us together: they remind me where I come from. I am grounded by them, but I am also lifted up and held together by the experience, wisdom and hope of those who came before me. Although, like anyone, I differ from my family in any number of ways, I draw strength from being part of a greater whole. The threads of family stories connect me to the past and, via my children, to the future. Whispering to my youngest in the bedtime hour, I think back to when I myself was five years old, lying in the cosy dark of the blue-wallpapered bedroom, listening to my mum's soothing voice telling me a bedtime story. I cannot remember a time before story. It runs through my blood and it is woven into the sinews of my body. Story is where I come from; story is who I am.

Writer and filmmaker Nora Ephron, in a speech that she gave at Wellesley College in 1996, offered the advice to 'above all, be the heroine of your life, not the victim'.[10] In the little stories of your life, as in your larger, overarching 'life story', you are the main character – the heroine or the hero. Living, and telling, the stories of our lives is, for each of us, a process of continuous learning and self-exploration. As we find our way through the world, we also find a way back to ourselves – we discover who we are. This is the storyteller's quest – to become the hero of your own life. Your voice matters because, in your life story, it is the voice of the heroine and you play the leading role. Your voice matters because your story matters and no one else can tell it but you. However quiet your voice may be, if your little stories are compellingly told, people will lean in closer to hear you. Taking control of your personal narrative can feel empowering; if you are in charge of your story, you are also, in a sense, in charge of your life.

An Ongoing Storytelling Practice

Establishing an ongoing storytelling practice means incorporating the recording and telling of little stories into your daily life. A bit of organization can make this manageable. Carry a small notebook in your bag or pocket so that you can jot things down to add to your journal later. Keep your journals organized by writing inside the front cover of each notebook the dates that its entries begin and end and by storing them chronologically on a shelf or in a box. In the same way, it's useful to have a folders system for your photographs. For example, I keep a folder on the desktop of my laptop into which I put one photograph of each of my children, each week. This makes it much easier for me to print photographs or make a photobook at a later date. You can organize your own photographs on a theme, time period (e.g. week/month) or by collecting one photograph from each day.

Periodically, do take the time to print your photographs. I confess that I am terrible at remembering to do this, but I am always delighted when I do and a packet of prints arrives through the post. You can frame or display the prints, send them to friends and family, stick them into albums or pop them directly into your journal. My friend, photographer Xanthe Berkeley[11], collects photographs into stacks, themed by event, period or subject. She adds a short, written explanation and ties up them with ribbon into simple but lovely time-capsules. You could equally store collections of your small stories in shoeboxes, or robust envelopes – choose a system that works best for you.

There are other benefits to telling the little stories of your life. An ongoing storytelling practice ensures that you preserve memories, both for yourself and for those close to you. In the same way that you tell everyday stories, you can also use storytelling to preserve a record of events, trips or special occasions. Storytelling has wider uses, too. For those with a small business, telling the stories of your life as they intersect with your business is a way in which to build up and connect with a customer base. When you tell the story of your brand, the same storytelling principles apply as when you tell the stories of your life. Storytelling can provide inspiration for creative work and you can use it to build a distinctive social media presence. To this end, aim to have a consistent style, look and feel to your images, one that is distinctive to your personal story. For me, this is muted colours, calm images of nature, negative space and pared-back styling; for you it may be quite different. Finding the storytelling style that best reflects you is a process. Creating a vision board, like the one in Chapter Three, can be a helpful way to consolidate your ideas of the mood that best reflects your social media storytelling. Learning to tell your little stories in a compelling way will draw people in to your life or – if you have one – your creative business. Whether it's a job interview, a date, or a conversation online, you can form genuine connections with people by sharing your little stories. On social media, as in real life, this connection is a two-way process – as you share your story with others, it's crucial to reach out and engage with the stories that they are telling you. Leave comments, ask questions, form friendships. Take a peek into the stories of others as you invite them to peer through the window into yours. Though our stories draw us inwards, they are also a path to connection.

Above all, storytelling is an act of archiving and memory-keeping. We collect together our little stories so that we can return to them in the future. Combined, our stories coalesce to become a message, a gift from our present selves for our future selves to pick up, re-read and relive. Over time as we collect together story fragments, themes and patterns begin to emerge. Look back over your photographs or flick through your journal. Are there noticeable threads woven through your words and images? Every life contains recurring themes and often hidden patterns. Sometimes, when we look closely, we observe signs and synchronicity which have meaning to us alone, such as the unexpected appearance of objects which remind us of someone we have lost. In the end, our stories will be what we ourselves leave behind – a personal legacy and a chapter of our family history. By collecting together your little stories you are both defining and creating yourself. You will find that through the creative process of telling them, and the act of looking back on them, you can develop a clearer understanding of what it means to be you.

In her essay *Why I Write*, Joan Didion describes being compelled to write about the pictures in her mind: irresistible images that 'shimmer around the edges'.[12] Luminous pictures like these are a manifestation of the urge to capture meaningful moments; the images that shimmer in our minds are the stories that we feel compelled to tell. It seems to me that this 'shimmer' can be a light that comes from moments of unexpected magic: of mystery, delight, surprise or truth. Whether you call it shimmer, or wonder, or everyday magic, the thoughts, images and instances that shine for us are stories that are crying out to be told. This is why we pay attention – so as not to miss that elusive shimmer – the alluring glow that whispers 'tell my story'.

Conclusion

We are our little stories and they are us. It can seem that big stories are the most important – overarching narratives and formative events – but when the fabric of our lives is unexpectedly altered, we come to realize that it was little stories that meant everything all along. When I look back through the fogged-up window of my past, at people and moments now altered or lost, it's the familiar, uneventful, quiet times I wish I could relive. The daily details that once seemed insignificant are the precious treasures that I long for. The way that my Yorkshire granny applied her rouge before she left the house; the songs that I sang in the village bus shelter with my teenage best friend; the tinkle of my babies' laughs; the scent, on June evenings, of the white roses that climbed the walls of my house; the taste of sweet, sticky grilled bananas from a roadside stall in Thailand; or the sound of my returning brother's skateboard wheels grinding across the grill above my parents' cellar.

Some of our little stories we want to share, to open to the world, even to shout from the rooftops, but some we want to fold secretly away and keep them close, as if worn in a locket next to the heart, to take out and carefully unfold when we need to be reminded of what matters most of all. We find ourselves in small stories: the fleeting instants, the everyday treasures, the tiny interactions, the ordinary days. Virginia Woolf once compared her diary to an old desk into which she threw 'a mass of odds and ends'. Over time, she hoped that these would coalesce into what she described as 'a mould transparent enough to reflect the light of our life'.[13] Woolf's odds and ends are like our little stories – we hope that, if we continue to collect them, then over time our little stories will come together into a clear shape that reflects back to us the light of our life, perhaps revealing to us a meaning of which we were previously unaware. I hope that your little stories will reflect back to you what the poet Hafiz of Shiraz described as 'the astonishing light of your own being'; little stories can show you who you are.

These beautiful, ordinary days are the days of our lives. The only moment we can ever be sure of is the one we are in – right now. We can sleepwalk through it dull-eyed, faces lit only by the glow from our phone screens, or we can choose to open our eyes wide; to step into the world, accept the invitation to be astonished and capture the story of what we see.

Life is real; let's pay attention. We have stories to tell.

Afterword

It's been almost a decade since I left behind my Bristol house and the neighbours with their apple tree. I live in the countryside now, in a small Gloucestershire town. As it happens, Gloucestershire is a cider county; orchards are plentiful here, and apple trees are so revered that they are blessed each winter in a traditional celebration called a wassail. There seems to be an apple tree in every other garden in our town. Each autumn, kind folk leave baskets of windfall apples outside their houses for passers-by, with signs reading 'Bramleys', 'free apples' or 'help yourself'. It's a kind tradition that makes windfalls taste all the sweeter.

As I walk home, I pass one of these baskets of apples and fill a bag with glossy fruit to be baked into a cake; a new twist on an old story. There are always more apples and there will always, always be more stories.

Bibliography

BOOKS

Batchelor, Stephen. *Secular Buddhism: Imagining the Dharma in an Uncertain World.* New Haven: Yale University Press, 2017

Bennett, Andrew, and Nicholas Royle. *An Introduction to Literature, Criticism and Theory.* Harlow: Pearson Education, 1999

Berger, John. *Ways of Seeing.* London: Penguin Books, 1972

Booker, Christopher. *The Seven Basic Plots: Why We Tell Stories* London: Bloomsbury, 2004

Borzello, Frances. *Seeing Ourselves: Women's Self-Portraits.* London: Thames & Hudson, 2016

Boyd, Brian. *On the Origin of Stories: Evolution, Cognition and Fiction.* London: The Belknap Press of Harvard University Press, 2009

Buster, Bobette. *Do Story.* Wales: The Do Book Company, 2013

Buster, Bobette. *Do Listen.* Wales: The Do Book Company, 2018

Cameron, Julia. *The Artist's Way.* London: Souvenir Press, 2020

Catmull, Ed. *Creativity Inc: Overcoming the Unseen Forces that Stand in the Way of True Inspiration.* London: Transworld, 2014

Csikszentmihalyi, Mihaly. *Flow: The Classic Work on How to Achieve Happiness.* London: Penguin Random House, 2002

Dahl, Roald. *The Minpins.* London: Puffin, 2013

Didion, Joan. *Slouching Towards Bethlehem.* London: 4th Estate, 2017

Dillard, Annie. *The Writing Life.* New York: Harper Collins, 1989

Eliot, T.S. *Collected Poems 1909–1962.* London: Faber & Faber, 1963

Elkin, Lauren. *Flâneuse: Women Walk the City in Paris, New York, Tokyo, Venice and London.* London: Vintage, 2016

Fassler, Joe (ed.). *Light the Dark: Writers on Creativity, Inspiration and the Artistic Process.* New York: Penguin Books, 2017

Feldman, Christina, and Willem Kuyken. *Mindfulness: Ancient Wisdom Meets Modern Psychology.* New York: The Guildford Press, 2019

Gay, Ross. *Catalog of Unabashed Gratitude.* Pittsburgh: University of Pittsburgh Press, 2015

Gay, Ross. *The Book of Delights.* Chapel Hill: Algonquin Books, 2019

Gilbert, Elizabeth. *Big Magic: Creative Living Beyond Fear.* London: Bloomsbury, 2015

Goldberg, Natalie. *Writing Down the Bones: Freeing the Writer Within.* Boulder: Shambhala, 2016

Gottschall, Jonathan. *The Storytelling Animal: How Stories Make Us Human.* New York: Mariner Books, 2013

Hạnh, Thích Nhất. *How to Walk.* London: Ebury, 2016

Hayes, Megan. *Write Yourself Happy: The Art of Positive Journalling.* London: Gaia, 2018

Kaufman, Scott Barry, and Carolyn Gregoire. *Wired to Create: Unravelling the Mysteries of the Creative Mind.* New York: Penguin Random House, 2016

Kenward, Joy. *The Joy of Mindful Writing.* London: Leaping Hare Press, 2017

Kephart, Beth. *Handling the Truth: On the Writing of Memoir.* New York: Avery, 2013

Lamott, Anne. *Bird by Bird.* New York: Anchor Books, 1994

Langer, Ellen J. *On Becoming an Artist: Reinventing Yourself Through Mindful Creativity.* New York: Random House, 2005

Manguso, Sarah. *Ongoingness: The End of a Diary*. London: Picador, 2019

McKee, Robert. *Story: Substance, Structure, Style and the Principles of Screenwriting*. London: Methuen, 1999

Oliver, Mary. *Devotions*. New York: Penguin Press, 2017

Oliver, Mary. *Upstream: Selected Essays*. New York: Penguin Random House, 2019

Patchett, Ann. *This is the Story of a Happy Marriage*. London: Bloomsbury, 2013

Rainer, Tristine. *The New Diary: How to Use a Journal for Self-Guidance and Expanded Creativity*. New York: Penguin Books, 2004

Rainer, Tristine. *Your Life as Story: Discovering the "New Autobiography" and Writing Memoir as Literature*. New York: Penguin Putnam, 1997

Sackville-West, Vita (ed. Mary Ann Caws). *Selected Writings*. New York: Palgrave Macmillan, 2003

Shapiro, Dani. *Still Writing: The Perils and Pleasures of a Creative Life*. New York: Grove Press, 2013

Solnit, Rebecca. *The Faraway Nearby*. London: Granta Books, 2013

Storr, Will. *The Science of Storytelling*. London: William Collins, 2019

Williams, Mark, and Danny Penman. *Mindfulness: A Practical Guide to Finding Peace in a Frantic World*. London: Piatkus, 2011

Wilson, E.O. *The Origins of Creativity*. Allen Lane, 2017

Woolf, Virginia (ed. Leonard Woolf). *A Writer's Diary: Being Extracts from the Diary of Virginia Woolf*. London: Persephone Books, 2012

Yorke, John. *Into the Woods: How Stories Work and Why We Tell Them*. London: Penguin Books, 2013

ARTICLES AND TALKS

Adichie, Chimamanda Ngozi. 'The Danger of a Single Story'. TED Talk, 2009 www.youtube.com/watch?v=D9Ihs241zeg

Backhaus, Jessica. 'Wonder'. www.fstoppers.com/video/jessica-backhaus-finds-beauty-and-wonder-ordinary-5208

Biswas-Diene, Robert. 'Your Happiest Days are Behind You'. TED Talk, 2014 www.youtube.com/watch?v=-QTVv9tAlIE

Didion, Joan. 'Why I Write'. *New York Times*, December 5th 1976 www.nytimes.com/1976/12/05/archives/why-i-write-why-i-write.html

Ephron, Norah. Commencement Address: www.wellesley.edu/events/commencement/archives/1996commencement

Erwitt, Elliott. Extract by Magnum Photos from *Museum Watching* (1999) www.magnumphotos.com/arts-culture/society-arts-culture/elliott-erwitt-life/

Evans, Diana. 'The Heart of The Matter'. *Harper's Bazaar*, August 2020

Feller, Bruce. 'The Stories That Bind Us'. *New York Times*, March 15th 2013 www.nytimes.com/2013/03/17/fashion/the-family-stories-that-bind-us-this-life.html

Fivush, Robyn. 'The "Do You Know?" 20 Questions About Family Stories'. www.psychologytoday.com/gb/blog/the-stories-our-lives/201611/the-do-you-know-20-questions-about-family-stories

Fivush, Robyn. 'What Stories Will You Leave as Your Family Legacy?'. www.psychologytoday.com/gb/blog/the-stories-our-lives/201911/what-stories-will-you-leave-your-family-legacy

Gaffney, David. 'Stories in your pocket: how to write flash fiction'. *The Guardian* 14th May 2012 www.theguardian.com/books/2012/may/14/how-to-write-flash-fiction

Gaiman, Neil. 'How Stories Last', speaking at Long Now Foundation, June 9th, 2015 www.brainpickings.org/2015/06/16/neil-gaiman-how-stories-last/

Gilbert, Elizabeth. 'Your Elusive Creative Genius'. TED Talk, 2009 www.ted.com/talks/elizabeth_gilbert_your_elusive_creative_genius

Glass, Ira. 'The Taste Gap: Ira Glass on the Secret of Creative Success, Animated in

Living Typography'. www.brainpickings.
org/2014/01/29/ira-glass-success-daniel-sax

Greenfield, Susan, Baroness Greenfield. 'On
Storytelling'. School of Life lecture, Conway
Hall, 11th December 2011 www.vimeo.
com/33716283

Jackson, Shirley. 'Memory & Delusion'. *New
Yorker* 31st July 2015 www.newyorker.com/
books/page-turner/memory-and-delusion

Lieberman, Matthew. 'Diaries: A Healthy
Choice'. *New York Times*, 21st December 2012
www.nytimes.com/roomfordebate/2012/11/25/
will-diaries-be-published-in-2050/diaries-a-
healthy-choice

Morris, William. 'The Aims of Art' (collected
in *Signs of Change* 1888). www.morrissociety.
blogspot.com/2010/10/william-morris-on-
happiness.html

Silverman, Sue William. 'Innocence &
Experience: Voice in Creative Nonfiction'.
www.creativenonfiction.org/brevity/craft/
craft_voice.htm

Wilson, Clare. 'Mindfulness and meditation
can worsen depression and anxiety'.
www.newscientist.com/article/2251840-
mindfulness-and-meditation-can-worsen-
depression-and-anxiety/

Winfrey, Oprah. Commencement Address
www.news.harvard.edu/gazette/story/2013/05/
winfreys-commencement-address/

STUDIES

Allen, Summer. 'The Science of Gratitude'.
(A white paper prepared for the John
Templeton Foundation by the Greater Good
Science Center at UC Berkeley, May 2018)
https://ggsc.berkeley.edu/images/uploads/
GGSC-JTF_White_Paper-Gratitude-FINAL.
pdf?_ga=2.205728730.856362745.15961
91338-325901936.1596191338

Brewster, Liz, and Andrew Cox. 'The
daily digital practice as a form of self-care:
Using photography for everyday well-
being'. *Health: An Interdisciplinary Journal
for the Social Study of Health, Illness and
Medicine*, 2018. https://journals.sagepub.com/
doi/10.1177/1363459318769465

https://www.lancaster.ac.uk/news/
articles/2018/daily-photography-improves-
wellbeing/

Diehl, Kristin, Gal Zauberman, and Alixandra
Barasch. 'How Taking Photos Increases
Enjoyment of Experiences'. *Journal of
Personality and Social Psychology*, 2016, Vol.
111, No. 2, 119–140

Duke, Marshall P., Amber Lazarus and
Robyn Fivush. 'Knowledge of family history
as a clinically useful index of psychological
well-being and prognosis: A brief report'.
*Psychotherapy: Theory, Research, Practice,
Training*, 2008. 45(2), 268–272. https://doi.
org/10.1037/0033-3204.45.2.268

Nezlek, John B., David Newman and
Todd M. Thrash, 'A daily diary study
of relationships between feelings of
gratitude and well-being'. *The Journal
of Positive Psychology*, 2016. DOI:
10.1080/17439760.2016.1198923

WRITERS AND PHOTOGRAPHERS
INTERVIEWED BY LAURA

Polly Alderton | www.dollyandfife.com

Bobette Buster | www.bobettebuster.com

Emma Christie | www.emmachristiewriter.
com/

Rachel Edwards | www.racheledwards.com

Dominique St-Germain | www.instagram.
com/karayiib/

Eliska Tanzer | www.hardmanswainson.com/
authors/eliska-tanzer/

Jo Yee | www.joannayee.com/

Endnotes

CHAPTER 1: THE MAGIC
OF THE EVERYDAY

1. Oliver, *Devotions (Sometimes)*
2. Shapiro, *Still Writing* p.123
3. Dillard *The Writing Life*, p.32
4. https://www.lancaster.ac.uk/news/articles/2018/daily-photography-improves-wellbeing/

CHAPTER 2: BEING IN
THE MOMENT

1. Oliver, *Upstream*, p.8
2. Csikszentmihalyi, *Flow*, p.33
3. Feldman & Kuyken, *Mindfulness*, p.14
4. Feldman & Kuyken, *Mindfulness*, p.17
5. Wilson, 'Mindfulness and meditation can worsen depression and anxiety'
6. Hạnh, *How to Walk*, p.19
7. Hạnh, p.71
8. Buster, *Do Story*, p.63
9. Sackville-West, *Selected Writings*, p.125.
10. Kenward, *The Joy of Mindful Writing*, p.13
11. Goldberg, *Writing Down the Bones*, p.36
12. Cameron, *The Artist's Way*, p.14
13. Batchelor, *Secular Buddhism* (http://blog.yalebooks.com/2018/03/10/meditation-and-photography)
14. Quoted in 'Dorothea Lange used photography to make an ugly world beautiful. She used words to give that beauty meaning.' Philip Kennicott, *Washington Post*, February 20th 2020
15. Hạnh, *How to Walk*, p.12
16. Manguso, *Ongoingness*, p.85

CHAPTER 3: LOOKING INWARDS

1. Didion, *Slouching Towards Bethlehem*, p.136
2. Rainer, *The New Diary*, p.19
3. Allen, 'The Science of Gratitude', p.4
4. Nezlek, Newman & Thrash, 'A daily diary study of relationships between feelings of gratitude and well-being'

5. Gay, *The Book of Delights*, p.1
6. Gay, p.11
7. Gay, p.108
8. Manguso, *Ongoingness*, p.77
9. Manguso, p.86
10. Backhaus, 'Wonder'

CHAPTER 4: THE MYSTERY
OF CREATIVITY

1. Langer, *On Becoming an Artist*, p.24
2. Wilson, *The Origins of Creativity*, p.3
3. Kaufman & Gregoire, *Wired to Create*
4. Gilbert, *Big Magic*, p.247
5. Gilbert, p.34
6. Gilbert, 'Your Elusive Creative Genius'
7. Csikszentmihalyi, *Flow*, p.41
8. Csikszentmihalyi p.74
9. Woolf, *A Writer's Diary*, p.220
10. Langer, *On Becoming an Artist*, p.211
11. Wilson, *The Origins of Creativity*, p.23
12. Cameron, *The Artist's Way*, p.21

CHAPTER 5: SEEING THINGS
DIFFERENTLY

1. Morris, 'The Aims of Art'
2. Buster, *Do Story*, p.22
3. Storr, *The Science of Storytelling*, p.28
4. Storr, p.29
5. Erwitt, Extract by Magnum from *Museum Watching*
6. Berger, *Ways of Seeing*, p.8
7. Berger, p.10
8. Goldberg, *Writing Down the Bones*, p.47
9. Goldberg, p.82
10. Lamott, *Bird by Bird*, p.100
11. Dahl, *The Minpins*
12. Jackson, 'Memory & Delusion'

CHAPTER 6: FINDING YOUR
CREATIVE VOICE

1. Winfrey, Commencement Address
2. Dillard, The Writing Life, p.68
3. Lamott, *Bird by Bird*, p.226
4. Gilbert, *Big Magic*, p.92
5. Solnit, *The Faraway Nearby*, p.4

CHAPTER 7: THE POWER
OF STORY

1. Storr, *The Science of Storytelling*, p.20
2. Greenfield, 'On Storytelling'
3. McKee, *Story*, p.12
4. Solnit, *The Faraway Nearby*, p.27
5. Patchett, *This is the Story of a Happy Marriage*, p.125
6. Boyd, *On the Origin of Stories*, p.393
7. Evans, 'The Heart of the Matter'
8. Storr, *The Science of Storytelling*, p.203
9. Adichie, 'The Danger of a Single Story'

CHAPTER 8: CRAFTING
LITTLE STORIES

1. Diehl, Zauberman & Barasch, 'How Taking Photos Increases Enjoyment of Experiences'
2. Brewster & Cox, 'The daily digital practice as a form of self-care'
3. Lieberman, 'Diaries: A Healthy Choice'

CHAPTER 9: YOUR STORY

1. Borzello, *Seeing Ourselves*, p.19
2. https://www.instagram.com/thisisjules/
3. Borzello, *Seeing Ourselves*, p.231
4. http://www.vivianmaier.com/gallery/self-portraits/
5. Eliot, *Collected Poems*, p.79
6. Duke, Lazarus & Fivush, 'Knowledge of family history as a clinically useful index of psychological well-being and prognosis'
7. Fivush, 'The "Do You Know?" 20 Questions About Family Stories'
8. Feller, 'The Stories That Bind Us'
9. Fivush, 'What Stories Will You Leave as Your Family Legacy?'
10. Ephron, Commencement Address
11. https://www.xantheberkeley.com
12. Didion, 'Why I Write'
13. Woolf, *A Writer's Diary*, p.14

Acknowledgements

My sincere thanks are due to the following people, without whom this book would not exist:

To my brilliant agent Caroline Hardman, I'm so thrilled to have you in my corner.

To the fantastic team at Quadrille; particularly my wonderful editors, Sarah Thickett and Harriet Butt, copy editor Sarah Mitchell, and designer Gemma Hayden, who perfectly understood my aesthetic and has put together a beautiful book.

To the writers and photographers who kindly shared their thoughts on creativity and storytelling: Polly Alderton, Emma Christie, Rachel Edwards, Dominique St-Germain, Eliska Tanzer and Jo Yee. Thank you.

To Beth Kempton, whose advice was invaluable, for both my book proposal and the writing life.

To Bobette Buster for giving her time and sharing her wisdom. It was truly an honour to speak to you.

To Chloe Turner, for our bookish conversations over toddler group coffee, and for showing me how to make space for writing in amongst the chaos. I can't wait to see my book on a shelf next to yours.

To Annie Marston, who humoured me when I suggested we create a knitting blog – all of this started there. You have always believed in me, you're the truest friend.

To my parents, whose love and support is a strong thread that runs through my own story and to my brother Tom – across the ocean, but in my heart.

To the family storytellers, Granny Tiger and Grandma Jean. From you, I learned where I come from, and who I want to be.

To everyone who has engaged with my story by reading my words or connecting with my photographs. Thank you for taking the time to peek into my everyday, and for sharing yours with me. I wrote this book for you.

Finally, to Dan and our three boys, who are everything to me. You fill my ordinary days with joy and wonder. Between us, we juggled lockdown, home learning and book deadlines. Thank you. I love you.

About the author

Laura Pashby is a writer and a photographer. She tells stories using words and photographs: online, for brands, and in magazines. She is also a qualified teacher with an MA in Literature, and she teaches storytelling E-courses. Laura spent three years as the deputy editor of *91 Magazine* – an independent creative living magazine. Across social media, but particularly on Instagram, she has an established and engaged following with an interest in her atmospheric imagery and soulful storytelling. She lives in Gloucestershire with her husband and three sons.

#littlestoriesbook

FIND LAURA HERE:

laurapashby.com

@circleofpines